To Des, in the year 00,

Viv & Val

xx

Swansea City Football Club

An A-Z

SWANSEA CITY FOOTBALL CLUB
AN A-Z

Dean Hayes

Aureus

First Published 1999

©1999 Dean Hayes
Cover photographs © South Wales Evening Post

Printed in Great Britain by Creative Print and Design (Wales).

A catalogue record for this book is available from the British Library.

Aureus Publishing 24 Mafeking Road Cardiff CF23 5DQ.

ISBN 1 899750 04 5

For Swans fans everywhere

Acknowledgments

I should like to express my thanks to the following organisations for their assistance:

Swansea City FC; The Association of Football Statisticians; The Football League Ltd; The British Newspaper Library; Swansea City Library; The Harris Library and Bolton and Blackburn Central Reference Libraries.

Thanks also to the following individuals: Ben Hayes; Iain Price; Harry Williams; Geraint Jenkins; Gareth Jones; and Paul Jones.

Bibliography
The Swansea City Story by Brinley Matthews
A Hundred Years of Welsh Soccer by Peter Corrigan (published by Welsh Brewers)
Swansea City 1912-1982 by David Farmer (published by Pelham Books)
Swansea Town Handbooks
Swansea City Programmes

Photographs
Photographs have been supplied by Lancashire Evening Post, Manchester Evening News, Liverpool Daily Post and Echo and the author's own personal collection.

ABANDONED MATCHES

An abandoned match is one which is called off by the referee when it is in progress, because conditions do not permit it to be completed.

A number of games at the Vetch have been abandoned because the ground was waterlogged or as in the FA Cup tie against Wealdstone in November 1986, a sudden torrential downpour of rain caused the referee to halt proceedings. The last game to be abandoned at the Vetch was on 28 February 1989 when the match against Huddersfield Town was abandoned with the Yorkshire side leading 1-0 because of a floodlight failure at half time!

ADAMS, MICKY

Micky Adams started his footballing career as an apprentice with Gillingham and turned professional in November 1979. After winning England Youth honours and appearing in 92 league games for the Kent club, he was transferred to Coventry City in the summer of 1983 for a fee of £75,000.

At Highfield Road, Adams was a virtual ever-present and scored nine goals in 90 league games before joining Leeds United in January 1987. He actually played for the Elland Road club against the Sky Blues in that season's FA Cup semi-final but was on the losing side. After 73 league appearances for Leeds he was sold to Southampton for £250,000 and in five years at The Dell clocked up 174 first team outings.

After being given a free transfer he had a brief spell at Stoke City before joining Fulham as player-coach. In February 1996 he was appointed as the club's player-manager, then the league's youngest. Though injuries restricted his appearances in 1996-97, he led the club to their first promotion since 1982 in his first full season in charge and fully deserved his election as Third Division Manager of the Year.

Surprisingly he was allowed to leave Craven Cottage in October 1997 and took over the reins at Swansea but after just 13 days in charge he walked out on the club after finding that money promised for new signings was not available.

He was then appointed manager of Brentford but in the summer of 1998 he left to become assistant-manager at Nottingham Forest.

AGGREGATE SCORE
Swansea's highest aggregate score in any competition came in the European Cup Winners' Cup of 1982-83. In the first leg at the Vetch Field against Sliema Wanderers of Malta, the Swans won 12-0 with no fewer than eight Swansea players getting their names on the scoresheet. In the return the Swans won 5-0 to notch up 17 goals without reply over the two legs.

ALLCHURCH, IVOR
Known as the 'Golden Boy of Welsh Football' he began his league career with his home-town club Swansea and made his debut in the local derby against Cardiff City on Christmas Eve 1949. Allchurch soon developed a fine understanding with Welsh international wing-half Billy Lucas and was soon capped himself when he played against England at Roker Park in November 1950.

Allchurch netted the first of seven hat-tricks for the Swans on 6 April 1953 against Brentford and his second 12 months later at Fulham. In 1954-55 Allchurch was the club's leading scorer with 20 goals including a hat-trick in the defeat of Ipswich Town on 4 December 1954, and the following campaign scored his fourth hat-trick at Notts County. When Derby County were beaten 7-0 on 8 April 1958 Allchurch netted a hat-trick and five months later scored four goals in a 5-0 win over Sunderland.

He was a fixture in the Welsh team, missing only a handful of games through injury. One of his best games for Wales was against a combined United Kingdom side for the 75th Anniversary of the Football Association of Wales when he scored twice in a 3-2 win. After he had appeared for

Wales in the 1958 World Cup Finals in Sweden, he received great praise from the World's Press and it was obvious that he would soon get the chance to show what he could do in the First Division.

He had scored 123 goals in 330 league games for the Swans when Newcastle United signed him for £27,000 in October 1958. When he arrived on Tyneside, the Magpies were struggling and he had to shoulder much of the club's attacking burden. He scored 51 goals in 154 games for the St James' Park club before leaving to join Cardiff City for £18,000.

His debut for the Bluebirds came in a 4-4 home draw against his former club Newcastle United and after scoring 12 goals in 35 games in that 1962-63 season, he was the club's top scorer for the next two campaigns. In 1963-64 he netted his first hat-trick for the club in a 3-3 draw at Sunderland and the following season scored a hat-trick in a 5-0 demolition of Swansea!

At the end of the 1965-66 season, Allchurch, who went on to win his 68th and last Welsh cap in 1966, moved back to Swansea for £6,000. Also in 1966, the Queen presented him with the MBE for his services to Welsh football. In 1967-68, his last season of league football, he netted his seventh and final hat-trick for the Swans against Doncaster Rovers. Remarkably the 38-year-old ended the campaign as the club's leading scorer with 21 League and Cup goals.

After leaving Swansea, for whom he scored 166 goals in 446 league games, he played non-league football for Worcester City, Haverfordwest and Pontardawe.

ALLCHURCH, LEN

Len Allchurch followed his brother Ivor by representing Wales Schoolboys and at the age of 14 after playing for Swansea Schoolboys he joined the Vetch Field ground staff where his older brother was in the first team.

He made his debut for the Swans at the age of 17 in April 1951 in a match against Grimsby Town, but it wasn't until he had served two years National Service in the Army that he established himself in the Swansea side.

When he was 21 he won the first of 11 full caps for Wales when he played against Northern Ireland in Belfast, forming a left-wing partnership with his brother Ivor. He had scored 49 goals in 272 league games for the Vetch Field club when in March 1961, Sheffield United paid £18,000 for his services.

3

In his first season at Bramall Lane he helped the Blades win promotion to the First Division, but in the summer of 1965 after appearing in 123 league games for the Yorkshire club he joined Stockport County for £10,000.

In 1966-67 he played an important role as the Edgeley Park club won the Fourth Division championship. Two years later after suggestion that he might move to Newport County, he returned to Swansea where he played out the remainder of his league career. He had scored 60 goals in 342 league games in his two spells with the club. In 1971 he joined his brother Ivor at Haverfordwest, later running a hotel in Swansea and establishing a successful leather goods business.

AMPADU, KWAME

Bradford-born Republic of Ireland Under-21 international 'Paddy' Kwame had played in Irish junior football with Sherrads United and Belvedere FC before joining Arsenal in the summer of 1988. In his three seasons at Highbury, Ampadu, a tricky winger, made only two league appearances, both as a substitute. In 1990-91 he enjoyed loan spells with Plymouth Argyle and West Bromwich Albion before subsequently joining the Baggies for £50,000 in June 1991. He had played in 62 games for Albion when he was transferred to Swansea for £15,000 in February 1994.

He excelled on the left side of the Swansea midfield with his aggressive attacking style of play. Ampadu was always on the look-out for goalscoring opportunities and often demonstrated his ability at dead-ball situations. Over the last couple of seasons he suffered with a series of niggling injuries and at the end of the 1997-98 season after which he had scored 15 goals in 178 League and Cup games, he was surprisingly released.

APPEARANCES

Wilf Milne holds the record for the greatest number of appearances in a Swansea shirt with a total of 657 games to his credit between 1920 and 1937. The total comprises of 585 league games, 44 FA Cup games and 28 Welsh Cup games. The long-serving full-back started a match in goal when goalkeeper Moore developed a knee injury on the way to Leicester and Milne volunteered to take his place in goal. He acquitted himself admirably in a goalless draw in what was his final season at the Vetch.

APPLETON, COLIN

Hard-tackling wing-half Colin Appleton began his Football League career with Leicester City and in 12 years at Filbert Street, scored 22 goals in 328 league games. Also during that time, Appleton captained the side in the FA Cup Final defeats of 1961 and 1963 and scored in the first leg of the 1965 League Cup Final. Unlucky not to win international recognition, he did represent the Football League against the Irish League in 1963.

He left Filbert Street in the summer of 1966 to join Charlton Athletic but a year later moved to Barrow as the Holker Street club's player-manager. After managing to keep them in the Third Division his health began to suffer and in January 1969 he left. Shortly afterwards he rejoined Scarborough for whom he had played prior to joining Leicester and in 1973 helped them win the FA Challenge Trophy.

In 1982 he returned to the Football League as manager of Hull City and proceeded to lead the Tigers to promotion to the Third Division. After taking the Yorkshire side very close to further promotion the following season, he resigned to take charge at Swansea.

He was only at the Vetch for seven months because in December 1984 with the Swans struggling at the foot of the Third Division, he was sacked.

After a short spell as Exeter City manager and a brief period in charge at Bridlington, he returned to Boothferry Park to manager Hull City for a second time. In October 1989 with the club in the lower reaches of the Second Division, he was dismissed.

ATTENDANCE - AVERAGE

The average home league attendances of Swansea City over the last ten seasons have been as follows:

1989-90	4,223	1994-95	3,582
1990-91	3,665	1995-96	2,996
1991-92	3,367	1996-97	3,850
1992-93	5,199	1997-98	3,443
1993-94	3,534	1998-99	5,225

ATTENDANCE - HIGHEST

The record attendance at the Vetch Field is 32,796 for the fourth round FA Cup game with Arsenal on 17 February 1968. Despite exerting a lot of pressure, the Swans lost 1-0 with the only goal of the game scored by Bobby Gould, former Welsh National team manager.

5

ATTENDANCE - LOWEST
The lowest ever attendance at the Vetch Field for a first team fixture was on 26 April 1976 when a crowd of just 1,311 turned up to see Swansea entertain Brentford in a Fourth Division game. For the record, the game ended all-square at 2-2.

ATTLEY, BRIAN
The son of a pre-war player, Len, Cardiff-born Brian Attley began his football career with his home-town club but was never really a regular first-team player at Ninian Park and left the Bluebirds in February 1979 to join Swansea for £25,000.

One of John Toshack's first signings, he made his debut for the Vetch Field club as a substitute in a 2-1 defeat at Exeter City. Playing mainly in a defensive role, usually at full-back, he was twice in promotion sides with the Swans, ending in the First Division. After failing to make the Welsh club's line-up for the historic opener in the top flight, he figured in only four matches before being transferred to Derby County for £25,000.

During his time at the Baseball Ground, he had a loan spell with Oxford United but at the end of the 1983-84 season after which he had appeared in 55 league games for the Rams, he went to play non-league football for Gresley Rovers.

AUTOGLASS TROPHY
The Autoglass Trophy replaced the Leyland Daf Cup for the 1991-92 season. The Swans lost their first preliminary round match 3-0 at Bournemouth and then played out a goalless draw at home to rivals Cardiff City in front of a Vetch Field crowd of 2,955 and so failed to qualify for the knockout stages.

In 1992-93, the Vetch side won both of its preliminary round matches, beating Exeter City 5-2 at St James' Park with Cullen, Wimbleton, West, Legg and Bowen the scorers and then Leyton Orient 1-0 with Colin West grabbing the all-important goal. In the second round, the Swans beat Cardiff City 2-1 but then went out of the competition, losing 3-2 after extra-time at home to Exeter City.

In 1993-94, the Swans again won both of their preliminary group matches to qualify for the knockout stages, beating Plymouth Argyle 3-1 at Home Park and then Exeter City at home 2-0. For the second year in succession, the Welsh club drew Exeter City in the knockout stages after beating them in their preliminary round matches, gaining revenge for the previous season's defeat with a 2-1 home win.

The Swans were drawn at home to Port Vale in the third round and beat the Valiants 1-0 with Chris Burns who was on loan from Portsmouth, the scorer. In the Southern Area quarter-final, a goal from Colin Pascoe was enough to beat Hereford United and take the Swans through to the Area semi-final against Leyton Orient at Brisbane Road.

The Vetch side turned in an outstanding performance winning 2-0 with goals from Torpey and Chapple. In the Southern Area Final, the Swans met Wycombe Wanderers over two legs. A crowd of 6,335 saw Swansea win 3-1 at the Vetch with two goals from Colin Pascoe and another from Jason Bowen giving them a two goal cushion for the second leg. Despite losing 1-0 at Wycombe's Adams Park Ground, the Swans went through to a Wembley final for the first time in their history where they met Huddersfield Town.

An early goal by Swansea's Andy McFarlane was equalised by Huddersfield's Logan and with the score after 90 minutes still level, the 47,733 spectators saw the two sides play out a further 30 minutes extra-time without any addition to the score. In the resultant penalty shoot-out, Roger Freestone the Swansea 'keeper made an excellent save and with two other efforts from the Yorkshire side hitting the bar, goals from John Cornforth, Kwame Ampadu and Steve Torpey gave Swansea the Autoglass Trophy.

AUTOWINDSCREEN SHIELD

Replacing the Autoglass Trophy for the 1994-95 season, the Swans won their opening match in the competition, beating Torquay United at Plainmoor 3-1 with two of their goals being scored by John Hendry, who was on loan from Tottenham Hotspur. In their other group match, Swansea were held to a 1-1 draw at the Vetch by Hereford United. In the second round, Hendry was on target again in a 1-0 win at Northampton, whilst goals from Hayes and Torpey gave the Swans a 2-1 victory at Oxford United in the Southern Section quarter-finals.

In the semi-finals, the Swans travelled to St Andrews to take on Birmingham City but after playing well to earn a 2-2 draw after extra-time, went out on the sudden death rule when Paul Tait struck the winner for the Blues. Tait in fact scored the winner for the St Andrews club against Carlisle United in the Wembley final.

In 1995-96, a Steve Torpey goal gave Swansea a 1-1 draw at Shrewsbury and though the club's home game in the group against Leyton Orient was goalless, the Vetch Field club went through to the knockout stages. In the second round they lost 1-0 at Peterborough United.

The following season the Swans were held to a 1-1 draw at home to Wycombe Wanderers, but after extra-time had failed to produce any further goals the game went to penalties which the Swans won 6-5. In the second round, Swansea lost 1-0 at home to Bristol City to a Gary Owers goal scored after just two minutes.

In 1997-98 the Swans received a bye into the second round but despite Matthew Bound giving them the lead in their match against Peterborough United, the Posh won the game 2-1 with their winner scored by Jimmy Quinn in the last minute!

In 1998-99, the Swans beat Barnet 4-1 at the Underhill Stadium with Tony Bird netting two of the club's goals but then went out in the second round, losing 1-0 at home to Gillingham.

AWAY MATCHES

Swansea's best away win in the Football League is 5-1, a scoreline inflicted upon Notts County on 24 September 1955 and Wolverhampton Wanderers on 14 September 1985. The club have also won four away matches in the league by 4-0, against Port Vale on 21 September 1931, Torquay United on 25 September 1948, Darlington on 22 January 1977 and Hartlepool United on 31 December 1977.

The Swans' worst league defeat on away soil is 8-1 at Fulham on 22 January 1938. The club have also lost 7-0 on three occasions during their travels - Tottenham Hotspur on 3 December 1932, Bristol Rovers on 2 October 1954 and Workington on 4 October 1965. Swansea last conceded seven goals on 30 August 1977 when they went down 7-4 at Hull City.

In cup games Swansea have suffered two 8-0 defeats: at Liverpool in a third round FA Cup tie on 9 January 1990 and against Monaco in a European Cup Winners' Cup first round second leg match on 1 October 1991.

AWAY SEASONS

Swansea's longest league run of undefeated away matches is 12 during the 1970-71 season when the club finished 11th in the Third Division. The club's longest sequence of away wins in the league is four, achieved in seasons 1955-56, 1987-88 and 1992-93.

B

BALL, BILLY

Though his Swansea career was brief, Billy Ball, who joined the Vetch Field club from Stoke in 1912, was the first soccer hero that the town knew.

In the club's first competitive game, a 1-1 draw against Cardiff, it was Billy Ball who scored the first goal for the Swans. He also went on to become the first Swansea player to be sent off, albeit for a minor offence!

Ball was a great favourite with the Swansea crowd who would shout 'Give it to Bally'. In fact, he was awarded an overcoat from Stewarts 'The King Tailors' on becoming the first Swansea player to score two goals in a home league match, doing so against Pontypridd in December 1912.

Also during that first season, he scored another two goals in the 4-2 Welsh Cup semi-final win over Cardiff, who were then leading the Southern League Second Division. The Swans went on to win the Welsh League title and Welsh Cup, defeating Pontypridd in the final with Ball's goals playing an important part.

BARCELONA FORMATION

On 12 March 1960, the club adopted 'The Barcelona Formation' for the first time for their match at home to Scunthorpe United. The Swans lined up with four full-backs, two half-backs and four forwards and beat their Lincolnshire opponents 3-1. But after only two successes in their next eight games, the system was dropped.

BARTLETT, JOHN

John Bartlett was appointed the secretary of Croydon Common in 1903 and four years later played a leading role when the club turned professional and joined the Second Division of the Southern League. He assembled a good squad of players and led the Robins to third place in their first season in the competition. They won promotion to the First Division in 1909 after finishing as champions but after giving way to Nat Whittaker, he left to take charge at Leicester Fosse.

Bartlett who was 34, was the youngest manager in the Football League, but his two seasons in charge at Filbert Street were difficult ones as the club struggled near the foot of the Second Division. He resigned his post in March 1914 after the club had been fined for making an illegal approach to an Ilford player by the name of Blake.

In May 1914 he joined Swansea as their manager after turning down an offer from the German FA to coach in that country. It proved to be a wise decision as a few months later, the first World War started. Bartlett left the Welsh club in 1915.

BARTLEY, DANNY

England Youth international Danny Bartley began his Football League career with Bristol City, making his debut as a substitute against Wolverhampton Wanderers in December 1965. He netted seven goals in 101 Second Division games before joining Swansea in a joint £10,000 deal with Dave Bruton in August 1973.

During his time at the Vetch Field, he was converted into an attacking left-back and formed a most effective full-back pairing with Wyndham Evans.

After helping the club win promotion to the Second Division, Bartley was one of the Welsh side's better players during the 1979-80 campaign as they ended the season in the higher league in mid-table. After scoring eight goals in 199 league games, he left the club in March 1980 to join Hereford United. He later played non-league football for Trowbridge Town, Forest Green Rovers, Maesteg Park, Port Talbot and Bridgend Town.

BEECH, CYRIL

The younger brother of Gilbert Beech, left-winger Cyril Beech joined Swansea from Merthyr Tydfil with his brother in 1950.

The pacy flanker was nicknamed 'Tulyar' after the famous racehorse and during his five year stay at the Vetch, he created a number of goals for his colleagues. However, he did find the target himself and in 133 league games he netted 34 goals.

In 1953 he left the Vetch to play non-league football for Worcester City but after a couple of seasons returned to the Football League to play for Newport County. He went on to score eight goals in 39 league games for the Somerton Park club before hanging up his boots.

BEECH, GILBERT

Nottingham-born Gilbert Beech played for Walsall for a couple of seasons before playing for Birmingham in the Works Association. His impressive performances led to Merthyr Tydfil manager Albert Lyndon inviting him for a trial and after a few games he accepted their offer to turn professional and played for the club for a short while.

His brother Cyril followed him to Merthyr and in 1950 they both joined the Vetch Field club.

Gilbert Beech had first caught the Swans' attention when he played for Merthyr in their 2-0 Welsh Cup Final victory over Swansea at Ninian Park in 1949. He joined them at the end of that season and went on to play for the club for the next ten years, appearing in 157 league games and scoring two goals from his position at full-back.

BENTLEY, ROY

Roy Bentley began his Football League career as an inside-forward with Newcastle United but when he joined Chelsea in January 1948, he was tried at centre-forward and with great success.

He captained the Stamford Bridge club to the League Championship in 1955 and in eight seasons with the Pensioners scored 128 goals in 324 league games. He appeared in the 1950 World Cup in Brazil and in 12 games for England scored nine goals. When he left Chelsea to join Fulham in September 1956, Bentley was converted to centre-half, a position which he also mastered with great success. After appearing in 143 league games for the Cottagers, he ended his playing career with Queen's Park Rangers before becoming Reading manager.

He soon reorganised the then Elm Park club and experimented on new methods of play. The Berkshire club finished consecutive seasons in fourth and fifth position in Division Three in 1967 and 1968 but after a poor season in 1968-69 he left the club.

Bentley took over at Swansea in August 1969 and at the end of his first season at the Vetch he had led the club to promotion to the Third

Division. After two seasons of mid-table placings, the Swans made a poor start to the 1972-73 campaign, and in October 1972 Bentley was sacked. He was unfortunate in that he had lost the services of two key players in Barrie Hole and Mel Nurse, and his major signing, Welsh international Ronnie Rees had failed to deliver the goods.

After managing non-league Thatcham Town, Bentley later held the post of secretary at both Reading and Aldershot.

BEST STARTS
Swansea have been unbeaten for the first seven games of a league season on four occasions - 1926-27; 1948-49; 1968-69 and 1978-79.

In 1923-24, the Swans started the season with five successive wins, finishing the campaign in fourth place in the Third Division (South).

BLACK FRIDAY
On 20 December 1985, Swansea City FC Ltd was 'wound up'. It was said that the club ceased to exist. However, a group of former Swansea directors worked so hard that permission was given for the Swans to play at Ninian Park against Cardiff City on Boxing Day. Though the Vetch Field club went down to a last minute goal, the Swansea supporters went home with their heads held high.

Over the next few months, the club made a number of visits to the High Court to keep league football alive at the Vetch.

In May 1986, Doug Sharpe and his team put their rescue package to the Welsh club's creditors and when the voting was 10-1 in favour of accepting his proposals, subject to High Court approval, Swansea City was alive again!

BOND, JOHN
John Bond made his name as an outspoken manager after a career as a full-back for West Ham United and Torquay United. At Upton Park he developed into a steady skilful defender who would read the game well and was a dead-ball expert, especially from the penalty spot. He won a Second Division championship medal with the Hammers in 1958-59 and an FA Cup winners' medal in 1964. At Torquay he helped them win promotion to the Third Division before his retirement.

He then went into management, first with Bournemouth, then Norwich City, winning success for both clubs.

In October 1980 he accepted an offer to join Manchester City, replacing

John Bond

Malcolm Allison and Tony Book after the Maine Road club had made a dreadful start to the season. They ended the campaign in mid table, reached the League Cup semi-finals and the FA Cup Final where they lost to Spurs. Bond stayed at Maine Road until February 1983 when he resigned.

In December 1984 after a short spell in charge of Burnley, he took over the reins at Swansea and at the end of his first season at the club, they just avoided relegation. In October 1985 with the Swans on the verge of bankruptcy, Bond lost his job but was only out of the game for a short time before becoming manager of Birmingham City.

Always attracting the attention of the media, he was fined by the FA in 1987 for allegedly bringing the game into disrepute following some unflattering remarks about the England coaching scene.

In January 1990 he was appointed manager of Shrewsbury Town but resigned at the end of the 1992-93 season after they failed to make the Third Division play-offs, losing the last game of the season to relegation-threatened Northampton Town.

BOWEN, JASON

Able to play in midfield or on the wing, Jason Bowen began his Football League career with the Swans and after a couple of outings as a substitute in 1990-91, made his full first team debut in a 2-1 FA Cup win over Cardiff City in November 1991.

With his speed taking him past defenders and into shooting positions, he became a great favourite with the Vetch crowd, and on 13 March 1993 he scored his first hat-trick for the club in a 4-2 home win over Chester City.

Already having been capped by Wales at Schoolboy, Youth, Under-21 and 'B' level, his form led to him winning his first full cap for his country when he played against Estonia in 1994. In 1994-95 he netted another hat-trick in a 7-0 Welsh Cup win over Taffs Well but in the close season after scoring 37 goals in 160 games he was transferred to Birmingham City for £350,000.

After making an immediate impact at St Andrews, scoring a number of spectacular goals, his progress was hampered by a series of unfortunate injuries.

When he recovered full fitness, he found himself out of favour and after a loan spell at Southampton, he joined Reading in December 1997 for a fee of £200,000.

BRACEY, LEE

Barking-born goalkeeper Lee Bracey began his career as a trainee with West Ham United, joining the Upton Park club in the summer of 1987. However, he failed to break into the Hammers' first team due to the outstanding form of Ludek Miklosko and signed for Swansea on a free transfer in August 1988. Over the next three seasons, he appeared in 128 first team games for the Vetch Field club, with all his league football being played in the Third Division.

Surprisingly, the Swans allowed him to leave the club in October 1991, Bracey joining Halifax Town for a fee of £47,500. When the Shaymen lost their Football League status at the end of the 1992-93 season, Bracey signed for Bury at a cut-price £20,000.

He shared the goalkeeping duties with regular custodian Gary Kelly but played no small part in helping the Shakers win promotion to the Second Division in 1995-96.

After a loan spell at Ipswich Town he joined the Portman Road club on a permanent basis for a fee of £40,000.

Lee Bracey

BRADSHAW, JOE

As a player, winger Joe Bradshaw made little impact at both Fulham and Chelsea but helped Southend United regain their place in the First Division of the Southern League. Bradshaw was player-manager at Roots Hall until the outbreak of the First World War but then left to join the army.

On his demob he was appointed manager of Swansea and almost immediately piloted the Swans into the Football League. In 1924-25 he guided the Welsh club to the Third Division (South) Championship and the following season, the club won through to the semi-finals of the FA Cup where they lost to Bolton Wanderers at White Hart Lane. Also that season, the Swans finished fifth in the Second Division.

He left the Vetch Field in May 1926 to manage Fulham but had a difficult time at Craven Cottage. The London club were relegated for the first time in their history in 1928 and though they scored 101 goals in 1928-29 and finished fifth in the Third Division (South), Bradshaw lost his job.

He then took charge at Bristol City, but in 1931-32 after only three victories in 32 matches he was sacked with the Ashton Gate club in a desperate financial position.

BROTHERS

There have been a number of instances of brothers playing for Swansea. The first pair of brothers that Swansea fielded were Tom and Len Emmanuel who started playing for the club just before the Second World War.

In 1952-53, three sets of brothers turned out for the club. Ivor Allchurch and his brother Len both gave the Swans great service. Ivor scored 166 goals in 446 league games during his two spells with the club and won 68 full international caps for his country. Len also represented Wales, playing in 11 internationals and he too had two spells with the club, scoring 60 goals in 342 league games. Both he and his brother were in a Swansea side in 1954 that played Luton Town and which was made up entirely of Welshmen.

Cyril and Gilbert Beech joined the Swans from Merthyr in 1950. Cyril Beech was a left-winger and scored 29 goals in 133 league games before joining Newport County in the summer of 1955. His brother Gilbert played all his league football at the Vetch Field appearing in 157 games.

Bryn and Cliff Jones were the third set of brothers that played for Swansea during the 1952-53 season. Bryn later played for a variety of clubs, whilst Cliff made 54 appearances for Wales as well as helping Spurs do the 'double' before ending his career with Fulham.

The following season, Colin and Alan Hole made their league debuts for the Swans, whilst younger brother Barrie joined the club from Aston Villa in 1970.

The last set of brothers to play for the Swans were Billy and Tony Screen. Both were capped for Wales at Under-23 level, Tony playing in 128 league games and Billy in 141 before the latter moved on to end his career with Newport County.

BROWN, W.Y.

During the 1919-20 campaign, the club's initial season in the First Division of the Football League, the Swans signed a player known by the name of W.Y. Brown. It seemed to be something of a strange signing, for Brown made his debut against local rivals Cardiff City at centre-half and yet it was the lack of goals that had forced the Vetch Field club into moving into the transfer market. However, towards the end of the season, he moved to centre-forward and began to strike up a prolific goalscoring partnership with Ivor Jones.

Brown was made club captain for Swansea's first season of League football in 1920-21 but had a fairly mediocre campaign which led to rumours that he would soon be retiring. Nothing was further from the truth and the following season he rediscovered his shooting boots and along with Jimmy Collins scored a hat-trick in an 8-1 win over Bristol Rovers at the Vetch on 19 April 1922, the first occasion that such a feat had been achieved by the club.

BRUTON, DAVE

Central defender Dave Bruton signed professional forms for Bristol City in July 1971 and made his league debut for the Ashton Gate club four months later at Sunderland. Over the next couple of seasons he only appeared in 17 league games, deputising for Dickie Rooks and David Rodgers before leaving to join Swansea in a joint £10,000 deal with Danny Bartley in the summer of 1973.

Under John Toshack, Bruton figured in successive promotion campaigns for the Swans before being released to join Newport County for a record £17,500 in October 1978. Bruton had scored 19 goals in 193 games for the Swans, and at Somerton Park he skippered the 1979-80 promotion-winning side.

After leaving Newport County he had spells at various non-league clubs including Gloucester City, Forest Green Rovers, Trowbridge Town,

Pontllanfraith, Caerleon, Cwmbran Town and Wootton Rovers where he
is player-manager.

BURGESS, RON

One of football's all-time greats, Ron Burgess arrived at Spurs in May 1936
as a forward and a year later was about to be released when he played for
the club's 'A' team as a late replacement. Spurs changed their minds and
offered him a place on the ground staff and an amateur contract at the
Northfleet Nursery.

He gained a first team place at right-half and within nine months of
making his debut, he was playing international football for Wales.
Throughout the war years he won representative honours for the RAF, FA
and his country, turning out for Spurs when service demands permitted, if
not 'guesting' for Notts County.

After the war he settled into the left-half position and captained Spurs
for eight consecutive seasons, leading them to the Second Division
Championship and the League Championship in successive seasons. He
was also captain of his country, winning 32 caps between 1946 and
1954. He was the first Welshman to play for the Football League, and
he played for Great Britain against the Rest of Europe in 1947.

In May 1954, shortly after making his final appearance for his country, he took the job of player-coach with Swansea, before graduating to
player-manager and then taking over the manager's job full time. The
Swans maintained their Second Division status during his term of office,
finishing tenth in three consecutive seasons. Burgess later moved to
Watford as manager and there discovered and transferred Pat Jennings to
Spurs.

BURNS, FRANK

Workington-born wing-half Frank Burns began his career as an amateur
with Wolverhampton Wanderers but after having failed to make the grade
joined Swansea in the summer of 1944.

When league football resumed in 1946-47, Burns was a virtual ever-present and when the club won the Third Division (South) Championship in
1948-49, there was only captain Reg Weston and himself who had not won
international recognition.

Burns went on to score nine goals in 172 league games for the Swans
before losing his place to 'Davo' Williams, and in the summer of 1952 he
left the Vetch to join Southend United. At Roots Hall, he was given a

more attacking role and scored 14 goals in 88 league outings before moving to Gresty Road and playing a further 30 league games for Crewe Alexandra.

BURROWS, FRANK

A tough, uncompromising defender, Frank Burrows began his football career with Raith Rovers before entering the Football League with Scunthorpe United in the summer of 1965. He went on to make 106 league appearances for the Irons before joining Swindon Town for a fee of £12,000 in 1968. He helped the Robins win promotion to Division Two as runners-up to Watford and to a shock League Cup Final victory over Arsenal in 1969. His playing career ended in October 1976 when after 298 league appearances for the Wiltshire club, he became Swindon's assistant-manager.

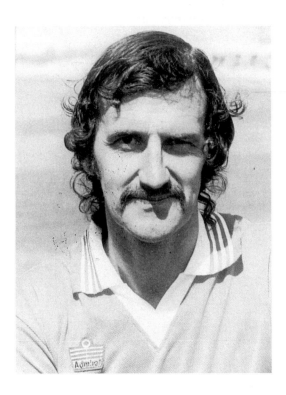

Frank Burrows

He later went into coaching but after joining Portsmouth in 1978, he succeeded Jimmy Dickinson as Pompey's manager, and in his first season in charge the club won promotion to the Third Division. He stayed until 1982 when he became coach at Southampton, later taking up a similar post with Sunderland.

He took over at Cardiff City in May 1986 as the Bluebirds entered the Fourth Division for the first time. The Ninian Park club were runners-up in 1987-88 but he left to work as assistant to John Gregory at Portsmouth. When Gregory left, Burrows took control of the club for a second time before becoming manager of Swansea in March 1991.

The Swans reached the Second Division play-offs in 1992-93 after a late run but lost 3-2 on aggregate to West Bromwich Albion in the semi-final stage. The following season he led the Vetch Field side to success in the Autoglass Trophy but in October 1995 he resigned his post. He returned to Ninian Park for a second spell as Cardiff manager in 1998, and in 1998-99 led them to promotion to the Third Division.

C

CALLAGHAN, IAN

Liverpool's most loyal servant, Ian Callaghan joined the Anfield club's ground staff in 1957 and made his debut against Rotherham United in April 1960.

Standing just 5ft 7ins, Callaghan began his footballing career as an outside-right but as the role of out-and-out winger disappeared he was converted into a midfielder.

In 21 years at Anfield, Callaghan played in a record 636 league games and a total of 843 games, winning every possible honour. He even played in the 1966 World Cup Finals and won a total of four England caps. He also holds the record gap between caps having played twice for England in 1966, he was not chosen again until October 1977, a gap of 11 years and 49 days.

He won European, League Championship and FA Cup winners' medals and was awarded the MBE as well as being voted the Football Writers' 'Player of the Year' in 1974.

He left Liverpool in September 1978 to join Swansea and made his debut in a 4-3 home win over Tranmere Rovers. In his first season with the Swans he helped them win promotion to the Second Division as they finished third in Division Three.

As the club consolidated their position in Division Two, Callaghan went on to equal Stanley Matthews' record by appearing in his 85th FA Cup tie at the age of 37 and a few weeks later established a new record when he appeared at Upton Park as the Swans played West Ham United.

Callaghan played in 76 league games for the Swans, his one goal being the only one of the match against Charlton Athletic in December 1979.

Ian Callaghan

CAPACITY
The total capacity of the Vetch Field in 1999-2000 was 11,477.

CAPTAINS
Among the many players who have captained the club are Jack Nicholas who the Swans signed from Derby County, and who led them in their pre-war Southern League days. During the 1914-15 season when the Swans defeated First Division Blackburn Rovers 1-0 in the FA Cup, they were captained by Joe Bulcock, who was later to lose his life during the hostilities.

The club's captain during 1920-21, the Swans' first season in the Football League, was W.Y. Brown, a centre-forward who netted the club's second hat-trick in the competition during an 8-1 win over Bristol Rovers.

Halfway through the club's Third Division (South) Championship winning season of 1924-25, Joe Sykes was made captain. Sykes who went on to appear in 313 league games for the Swans was an inspirational leader, and in 1925-26 helped the club reach the FA Cup semi-finals where they were beaten 3-0 by Bolton Wanderers.

When Swansea won the Third Division (South) Championship for a second time in 1948-49, they were captained by Reg Weston. A solid and reliable one-club man, Weston was a great leader and made 227 league appearances for the Swans before hanging up his boots.

When the Swans reached the FA Cup semi-final for the second time in their history in 1964, they were led by Mike Johnson. But despite taking a first-half lead they went down 2-1 to two second-half goals.

John Cornforth captained Swansea to success in the Autoglass Trophy Final at Wembley on 24 April 1994. The Welsh international scored one of the goals from the penalty-spot after the game had finished 1-1 after extra-time.

CARDIFF CITY
The club's arch rivals are Cardiff City and as most Swansea fans will know, they were the club's opponents in their first competitive game on 7 September 1912 at the Vetch Field. In fact, that was Swansea's first ever first team game as a professional outfit, and they drew 1-1 on the clinker surface. The return at Ninian Park later in the season was goalless.

The two clubs first met in the Football League on 5 October 1929 at Ninian Park in a game that was also without a goal. The Swans won the return at the Vetch on 8 February 1930, 1-0.

The club's first Welsh Cup competition match after entry into the

Football League took place at Ninian Park in April 1923; a match the Bluebirds won by the odd goal in five. The two sides next met at the Vetch in March 1925 with the Swans winning 4-0.

Swansea's biggest victory over Cardiff City came at the Vetch on Christmas Eve 1949 when goals from Billy Lucas (2), Jackie O'Driscoll (2), and Sam McCrory helped the Swans win 5-1 in front of a crowd of 27,264. City's revenge came in 1964-65 when in one of the final games of that campaign they won 5-0 with Ivor Allchurch scoring a hat-trick and John Charles the other two goals.

The clubs have met twice in the FA Cup with the Swans winning on both occasions and once in the League Cup when the Vetch Field club won 4-3 on aggregate.

The two clubs continued to meet in the Welsh Cup, many of the meetings producing memorable games. On 25 February 1960, the Bluebirds fielded their reserve team in a sixth round tie at the Vetch Field because the Welsh FA refused to change the date of the match, even though Cardiff had an important league match at Leyton Orient two days later. Swansea fielded their full-strength line-up but they soon went behind to a Steve Mokone goal. As the game wore on, tempers became frayed and the tackles more vigorous, but to the Swans dismay, Harry Knowles put Cardiff 2-0 with just 15 minutes to play. The Swans pulled a goal back before Colin Hudson was sent off for dangerous play. A few minutes later, the Bluebirds were reduced to nine men and Swansea ten, when Mokone and Harry Griffiths were dismissed after throwing mud at each other! The Ninian Park side hung on to win 2-1 but they were fined £350 by the Welsh FA and ordered to play their strongest side in the Welsh Cup in future.

In the 1965-66 Welsh Cup competition, the teams had drawn 2-2 at the Vetch Field and returned to Ninian Park for the fifth round replay. With just eight minutes of the second half played, Cardiff were 3-0 up and seemingly coasting into the next round. However, in the 64th minute, the game turned on its head when Don Murray the Bluebirds' centre-half received his marching orders. Within a minute, the Swans had pulled a goal back through Todd, who later netted a second and after Herbie Williams had equalised the game went into extra-time. Further goals from McLaughlin and Evans gave the Swans a remarkable 5-3 win.

One of the most emotional meetings between the two clubs as far as Swansea supporters are concerned was the first ever meeting in the Third Division on Boxing Day 1985, after the Vetch Field club had escaped the clutches of the Official Receiver. Had that game not been played then

Swansea City FC would not exist today. Though the Swans lost an evenly fought match to a late goal, every Swansea fan went home happy because the club was alive again!

In 1998-99 Swansea beat Cardiff City 2-1 at the Vetch with goals from Bound and Thomas and then picked up a point in a goalless draw at Ninian Park on 18 April 1999.

Below are Swansea's statistics against Cardiff:

	P	W	D	L	F	A
Southern League	4	1	2	1	3	3
Welsh Cup	33	7	8	18	42	62
Football League	42	16	13	13	56	52
FA Cup	2	2	0	0	4	1
League Cup	2	1	0	1	4	3
Autoglass Trophy	1	0	1	0	0	0
Freight Rover Trophy	1	1	0	0	2	0
Sherpa Van Trophy	1	0	0	1	0	2
TOTAL	86	28	24	34	111	122

CENTURIES
There are four instances of individual players having scored 100 or more league goals for Swansea. Ivor Allchurch is the greatest goalscorer in his Vetch Field career with 166. Other centurions are Robbie James (115), Herbie Williams (102), and Jack Fowler (100).

Andrew Legg and Alex Ferguson hold the record for the most consecutive league appearances - 108, although Legg holds the record for all games with 136.

CHAMPIONSHIPS
Swansea have won a divisional championship on two occasions. Despite beating Swindon 2-0 in the opening game of the 1924-25 season, the Swans' results over the next few weeks were mixed. On 27 September 1924 the Welsh club beat Charlton Athletic 6-1 with Jack Fowler setting an individual scoring record for a league match by scoring five goals - a record that still stands today. On that day the All Blacks were playing at St Helen's and the crowd for the Charlton game was less than half the 20,000 that had seen the opening game of the season.

The club's away form was poor yet at the Vetch, results were encouraging and on 8 November they beat Brentford 7-0 with Len Thompson (4) and Harry Deacon (3) both grabbing hat-tricks. It was after this demolition of the Griffin Park club that the Swans began to hit top form. By the end of the year Swansea were top of the league, having beaten league leaders Plymouth Argyle at the Vetch.

On 14 March 1925, the Swans travelled to Brentford who were struggling at the foot of the Third Division (South) and though most Swansea fans thought the two points were in the bag, the Bees gained revenge for their drubbing earlier in the season by winning 3-1. There were many who feared that the club's form would slump as it had the previous season, but when the Swans visited Home Park for the crucial game against Plymouth Argyle, they held a one point advantage over the Pilgrims with three games to play.

Despite going behind early in the game, the Swans equalised through Harry Deacon in the second-half and came away with a point. Plymouth then won their midweek game to go one point ahead of Swansea but only had game to play whilst the Swans had two. The Vetch Field club then beat Reading but Argyle won their final match of the season leaving Swansea needing to win their last game as the Devon club had a superior goal average. The Swans' opponents were Exeter City, but goals from Jack Fowler and Len Thompson gave the Welsh club a 2-1 win and the Third Division (South) Championship.

The club next won a divisional championship in 1948-49 when they once again won the Third Division (South) title.

In contrast to the previous Championship-winning season, the Swans made a good start and by the end of September were top of the league. Then came the club's first defeat at Leyton Orient but there were extenuating circumstances as Billy Lucas was injured before half-time and the Swans had to play with ten men. Then came a run of six consecutive victories in which 20 goals were scored and only one conceded including four by Stan Richards in the win over Swindon Town. Richards in fact was to end the season as the club's top scorer with 26 goals in 32 games - a remarkable achievement considering that he had a history of knee problems and could not always train properly because of the recurring injury.

In February 1949 the Swans beat Torquay United 6-1 with Sam McCrory scoring a hat-trick, it was a result which took the club six points clear at the top of the table. By the end of the following month, the Welsh club had extended their lead at the top by a further point and after winning at Brighton, the Championship was theirs with five games still to play.

The club went on to finish the season seven points ahead of runners-up Reading and were undefeated at home, dropping just one point. Over the season they established a number of records - 17 home wins in succession, six away wins in a row, 27 wins during the season and the most points (62) that had been gained in a season.

CHAPPLE, SHAUN

Shaun Chapple joined the club as a trainee in the summer of 1991. In his early days with the Swans, he struggled to hold down a regular first team place but following a successful loan period at Barry Town, he returned to show some excellent touches in midfield and establish himself in the Swansea side. He also earned some good reviews when he represented Wales at Under-21 level and was capped at 'B' international level.

A good passer of the ball, he scored some vital goals for the Vetch Field club, although the influential midfielder was forced to miss a number of games due to a cartilage operation and a bad leg injury suffered at Hartlepool United during the 1996-97 season. He had taken his total of first team appearances to 135 when in October 1997 he was allowed to join non-league Merthyr on a free transfer.

CHARLES, JEREMY

Son of Mel Charles and nephew of the legendary John Charles, he made his league debut for the Swans before his 17th birthday. The first game of the 1976-77 season was a League Cup tie against Newport County. Jeremy Charles came on as a substitute for Robbie James and scored twice in a 4-1 win, his first coming after he had been on the field for just two minutes. He ended his first season with the club with 23 goals.

Charles was a regular member of the Swansea side that rose from Division Four to Division One in four seasons. After helping the club win promotion from the Third Division, he scored the all important third goal in the 3-1 win at Preston North End in the final game of the 1980-81 season to take Swansea into the First Division for the first time in their history.

It was Charles who scored the club's first ever goal in Division One when he netted against Leeds United in a 5-1 win, but he missed quite a few matches during that 1981-82 season as he underwent two cartilage operations. During his time at the Vetch Field, Swansea received a number of offers for Charles from top flight clubs but refused all overtures until November 1983 when he was transferred to Queen's Park Rangers for £100,000.

Charles had scored 53 goals in 247 league games for the Swans but only stayed at Loftus Road a short time before joining Oxford United and helping them win the Second Division Championship in 1984-85. Injury brought his career to a premature end, his last league appearance coming against Arsenal at Highbury when he was sent off! Charles is now back at Vetch Field as one of the club's Football Development Officers.

Jeremy Charles

CHARLES, MEL

After a trial with Leeds United Mel Charles signed professional forms for Swansea Town in May 1952, and over the following seven seasons scored 69 goals in 233 league games including four in a 5-1 home win over Blackburn Rovers on the opening day of the 1956-57 season.

Though never the star that his elder brother John was, Mel Charles was a very good footballer, winning 31 full caps for Wales. He made his debut for his country against Northern Ireland in 1955 when playing at right-half but with typical versatility he also played at centre-half, inside-right and centre-forward. He was voted the best centre-half in the 1958 World Cup Finals but also showed his attacking qualities when he scored all four goals in Wales' 4-0 defeat of Northern Ireland in April 1962.

By this time Charles had become much sought after and in March 1959 he had joined First Division Arsenal for £42,750 plus David Dodson and Peter Davies. He made his Arsenal debut at centre-half against Sheffield Wednesday in August 1959 but his progress was hampered by a cartilage operation. In 1960-61, a second cartilage operation was required which resulted in him playing in only 19 league matches. In 1961-62 he started the season as the club's first-choice centre-forward scoring 11 goals in the first 18 games. He then lost his place to Geoff Strong and in February 1962 he was transferred to Cardiff City for £20,000.

Eventually displaced by his brother John on his return from Italy, he enjoyed a short but highly successful period with Welsh League side Portmadoc before returning to League action with Port Vale at the end of the 1966-67 season.

On his retirement he went into business in Swansea but was soon guiding the fortunes of his son Jeremy who played league football for Swansea City, Queen's Park Rangers, Oxford United and Wales.

CLEAN SHEET

This is the colloquial expression to describe a goalkeeper's performance when he does not concede a goal. Welsh international 'keeper Tony Millington had 20 clean sheets in 1969-70 when the Swans won promotion after finishing third in Division Four.

CLODE, MARK

A former trainee with Plymouth Argyle, Mark Clode joined Swansea on a free transfer in the summer of 1993 and made his debut at York City on the opening day of the 1993-94 season. His attacking bursts from the full-back position during his first season with the club culminated in him signing a three-year contract at the end of the 1993-94 campaign in which he played 42 League and Cup games including a memorable performance in the Autoglass Trophy Final at Wembley. Following a two-month period on the sidelines with a shin injury, the talented defender soon regained his first team place in 1994-95 and showed excellent attacking form, coupled with tigrish tackling.

Over the last few seasons his progress has been hampered by ham-string problems and a broken ankle sustained in a reserve team game. He had just returned to first team action at the start of the 1997-98 sea-son when he had to return to hospital for surgery on a shin problem that had been troubling him for a while. His comeback was delayed even further by an operation to remove an appendix in March 1998. Swansea fans will be hoping that it won't be long before he adds to his total of 146 first team appearances.

COATES, JONATHAN

Welsh Youth international Jonathan Coates joined the Swans as a trainee in the summer of 1993 and made his first team debut the following season in a 3-1 defeat at Fulham when he came on as a substitute for Darren Perett. During his first few seasons at the Vetch, he found his first team opportunities limited, even though he was a regular goalscorer at reserve team level.

In 1995-96 he was capped for the Wales Under-21 side against Moldova and Germany, yet at the end of the campaign he was rather surprisingly offered a free transfer by the club. Thankfully he remained at the Vetch and the following season became a first team regular, winning two more caps at Under-21 level even though he was dismissed in the match against Holland for two bookable offences.

Despite continuing to show excellent form on the left hand side of mid-field, he was switched to the left wing-back role in 1997-98 where his per-formances led to him being selected for the Welsh 'B' squad to play their Scottish counterparts. Coates who has scored 12 goals in 164 games for the Swans, had to withdraw due to injury.

COLEMAN, CHRIS

Swansea-born Chris Coleman joined his home-town club from Manches-ter City juniors in September 1987 and in his first season with the Swans helped them win promotion to the Third Division via the play-offs. He also won Welsh Cup winners' medals in 1989 and 1991 but after four sea-sons at the Vetch in which he appeared in 196 first team games, he left to join Crystal Palace for a fee of £275,000.

At Selhurst Park, Coleman won the first of 19 full caps for Wales when he played against Austria in 1992 and went on to appear in 190 games for the Eagles in a four-year stay with the London club.

In December 1995 he signed for Blackburn Rovers for £2.8 million and though he took a little time to settle in alongside Colin Hendrey in the heart of the Blackburn defence, he improved rapidly as the season progressed. However, in 1996-97 an achilles tendon injury reduced his number of appearances and when Roy Hodgson became manager at Ewood Park, Coleman did not figure in his plans, and after appearing in only 32 games he was allowed to join Kevin Keegan's Fulham for £2.1 million. In an impressive first season at Craven Cottage, he was voted by his fellow professionals into the PFA award-winning Second Division team, before helping them win the Second Division Championship in 1998-99.

Chris Coleman

COLLINS, JIMMY

Scottish half-back Jimmy Collins was signed by the Swans whilst serving in the army in mid Wales.

During the 1921-22 season, as the club went through a number of permutations in an attempt to find a winning line-up, Collins was tried at centre-forward in the match against Bristol Rovers and responded with a hat-trick in an 8-1 win, though he only managed seven league goals in a Vetch Field career spanning ten years.

By 1923-24, Collins had become the club's captain but early the following season, a campaign in which Swansea won the Third Division (South) Championship, Collins suffered a serious knee injury. Even when he did return later in that campaign, he was suspended along with Bennett for a 'serious breach of club discipline'.

Towards the end of the 1924-25 season, Collins was barracked by a section of the Vetch Field crowd, and in one game when the Scot was injured following a heavy tackle, some so-called Swansea supporters actually cheered at the player's misfortune.

Immediately after the game, Collins asked for a transfer but then decided to stay and fight. In fact, his performances led to him being the target of a number of top clubs.

He went on to appear in 274 league games for the club before hanging up his boots at the end of the 1929-30 season.

COLOURS

Although there were occasions in the 1930s and 1970s when the Swans wore black shorts to accompany their white shirts, they have in the main always played in an all-white strip.

The club's present colours are white shirts with maroon and black facing, white shorts with maroon and black trim and white stockings with maroon ring top. The Swans' change colours are maroon shirts with black and white facings, maroon shorts with black and white trim and maroon stockings with white band.

CONSECUTIVE HOME GAMES

Swansea have played a sequence of four home games in succession on a number of occasions but in 1992-93, they did so in just 11 days! The Swans not only fielded the same team but won all four games without conceding a goal as they won their way through to the play-offs.

Date	Opponents	Score	Scorers
17 April '93	Rotherham United	2-0	McFarlane; Cornforth
20 April '93	Huddersfield Town	3-0	Walker; Harris; Legg
24 April '93	Hartlepool United	3-0	Walker; Legg; McFarlane
27 April '93	Preston North End	2-0	Harris; McFarlane

CONSECUTIVE SCORING - LONGEST SEQUENCE

Ivor Allchurch holds the club record for consecutive scoring when he was on target, including the FA Cup tie at Wolverhampton Wanderers, in nine consecutive matches during the 1956-57 season.

CORK, ALAN

Alan Cork came through the Derby County ranks prior to turning professional for the Rams in the summer of 1978. However, he was never picked for the Derby first team and made his league debut whilst on loan to Lincoln City. He left the Baseball Ground on a free transfer and joined Football League newcomers Wimbledon.

'Corky' as he is affectionately known, top-scored for the 'Dons' in seasons 1978-79, 1980-81 and 1983-84 when Wimbledon won promotion to the Second Division. Though a broken leg kept him out of first team action for almost two years, he returned to win an FA Cup winners' medal in 1988 when Wimbledon unexpectedly beat Liverpool 1-0. Towards the end of his career at Wimbledon he became a valuable squad player, but in March 1992 after scoring 168 goals in 510 games he followed his manager Dave Bassett to Sheffield United.

He enjoyed cult status at Bramall Lane where he was mainly used as a substitute to be thrown into the fray when required. After leaving the Blades he joined Fulham, taking charge of the youth team before being appointed first team coach.

After becoming Swansea's assistant manager he replaced Micky Adams as the Welsh club's boss in October 1997 after the former had walked out on the club. Cork led the Swans to 20th position in the Third Division before being replaced by the club's current manager John Hollins.

CORNFORTH, JOHN

John Cornforth joined Swansea from Sunderland for a fee of £50,000 in the summer of 1991 after loan spells with Doncaster Rovers, Shrewsbury Town and Lincoln City. He recovered after breaking his leg to become a major influence in the Swansea midfield. He became the first Swansea captain in the history of the club to lead a team out at Wembley in the Autoglass Trophy Final against Huddersfield Town where he scored Swansea's first goal in the penalty shoot-out. His outstanding passing skills led to him winning full international honours for Wales in 1995 when he played against Bulgaria and Georgia.

In 1995-96, Cornforth suffered a bad knee injury, his absence coinciding with the club's slide down the Second Division table and eventual relegation. He had scored 18 goals in 193 games for the Swans when he was allowed to join Birmingham City for £350,000 in March 1996.

Unable to establish himself at St Andrews, he was transferred to Wycombe Wanderers but in 1997-98 when a further payment of the £50,000 fee was due to Birmingham City, he was dropped. A proposed return to Swansea broke down and though Cornforth had a loan spell at Peterborough United, he ended the campaign playing in Wycombe's final few games.

CRICKETERS

The only real cricketer of note to have played league football for the Swans is Jim Pressdee. A Welsh Schoolboy soccer international, he was on the staff of Swansea Town Football Club but at 16 years and 23 days, he became Glamorgan's youngest post-war cricketer.

A right-hand batsman and slow left-arm bowler, he topped the county bowling averages with 72 wickets at 19 runs each and held 42 catches in the leg trap in his first full season in 1955. Over the next few years, Pressdee's batting developed and in 1959 he made his maiden first-class century and topped the 1,000 run mark for the first time. His best season for the county was 1963 when he completed the 'double', scoring 1,435 runs at 34.17 and taking 104 wickets at 21.04 runs apiece. Pressdee who appeared in eight league games for the Swans went on to score 13,411 runs and capture 405 wickets before leaving county cricket in the summer of 1965.

CROWD TROUBLE

However unwelcome, crowd disturbances are far from a modern phenomenon at major football matches. Behaviour at the Vetch Field has usually been of a high standard and though Swansea supporters are well renowned for voicing their opinions at suspect referees, the occasions when their demonstrations boil over beyond the verbal are very rare indeed.

However, one such occasion did take place in the club's first season of League football in 1920-21. The crowd disturbance at the Vetch only ceased when Ben Watts-Jones the Swansea chairman and a police sergeant had gone to speak to the supporters. It was around this time that the Crystal Palace and Millwall grounds had been closed for two weeks as a result of crowd trouble and there were fears that the Vetch Field would go the same way as a number of Swansea 'supporters' continually hurled abuse at both sets of players!

CULLIS, KEITH

When millionaire mystery man Michael Thompson emerged as the new 'owner-elect' of Swansea Football Club, he promised that he would bring in a manager of quality. The Swansea fans were delighted with the news but when the chairman-elect appointed Keith Cullis, a manager without Football League experience, they were dismayed.

The Swans under Cullis and his assistant Paul Molesworth went five games without a win and failed to score in any of those games. Chairman Doug Sharpe was out of the country but returned immediately and appointed Jan Molby as the club's new player-manager.

CURTIS, ALAN

A nephew of former Swansea, Manchester City and Welsh international Roy Paul, he joined the Vetch Field club straight from school. After making his debut against Charlton Athletic in the final game of the 1972-73 season, Curtis quickly emerged as a first team player of imagination, skill and vision and a quite prolific marksman. He netted his first first team hat-trick in a 4-1 Welsh Cup win over Newport County in January 1977 and ended the season with 14 league goals. His first league hat-trick came in a 5-0 win over Crewe Alexandra on 12 November 1977. On 1 April 1978 both Curtis and Robbie James scored hat-tricks as the Swans recorded their biggest-ever league win, defeating Hartlepool United 8-0.

In May 1979, Curtis joined First Division Leeds United for £350,000 but his time at Elland Road was blighted by injury and loss of form.

He was soon back at the Vetch Field, because in December 1980 the Swans paid £165,000 to take him back to South Wales. In his first game with the Swans in his second spell, he scored the only goal of the game from the penalty spot against Watford. He went on to be an important member of the Swansea side that won promotion to the First Division for the first time in the club's history.

A regular for Wales, Curtis left the Vetch for a second time in

November 1983 following the club's relegation from the top flight. He joined Southampton for £85,000 to ease the Swans' financial plight. He failed to show his best form at The Dell and after a short loan spell at Stoke City, returned to South Wales to play for Cardiff City on a free transfer.

Capped 35 times by Wales, Curtis returned to his old stomping ground at Swansea for a third time in October 1989. He announced his retirement at the end of the 1989-90 season after having scored 96 goals in 364 league games. He then joined Barry Town as player-coach in the summer of 1990 before signing for Haverfordwest County in July 1991. Curtis is now back at the Vetch as assistant-manager to John Hollins.

Alan Curtis

D

DAVIES, ALAN

The aggressive midfielder began his Football League career with Manchester United and made his debut for the Red Devils against Southampton at Old Trafford on 1 May 1982. He looked to have a bright future with United but things did not materialise in quite the way the club and player had wished, although he did win an FA Cup winners' medal in 1983. Soon after the final against Brighton he broke an ankle and in the summer of 1985 he left Old Trafford to join Newcastle United. He never really settled at St James' Park and after loan spells with Charlton Athletic and Carlisle United, he signed for Swansea in July 1987.

After making his debut in a 2-0 win over Stockport County on the opening day of the 1987-88 season, he was a virtual ever-present at the Vetch Field for two seasons before leaving to join Bradford City. But after just one year at the Valley Parade, he returned to Swansea where he took his tally of goals to 12 in 127 league games.

The winner of 11 full caps for Wales, Davies died in tragic circumstances on 4 February 1992 when he was found dead in his fume-filled car.

DAVIES, DAI

Born in the South Wales mining village of Ammanford, goalkeeper Dai Davies began his career in local football before joining Swansea. He made his debut for the Swans against Third Division champions Chesterfield in the final game of the 1969-70 season. His first game in 1970-71 was against

Dai Davies in action

Preston North End, a match the Welsh side drew 1-1, before going on to complete a remarkable sequence of 19 matches undefeated to equal the club record set some ten years earlier.

In December 1970 he signed for Everton for £25,000 but after spending virtually four seasons in the shadow of Gordon West and his understudy David Lawson, Davies went back to the Vetch Field on loan. He returned to Goodison and went on to appear in 94 games before leaving to join Wrexham. Whilst with Everton he gained the first of 52 Welsh caps when he played in Wales' 2-1 win over Hungary in Budapest.

In his first season at the Racecourse Ground, Wrexham suffered the lowest number of defeats in their history as they won the Third Division Championship. In 1978-79 Davies helped establish the club's best-ever league defensive record of 42 goals conceded. At the end of the 1980-81 season Davies returned to play for Swansea in the top flight, where he was unbeaten in six consecutive matches. He had played in 77 league games before becoming player-coach at Tranmere Rovers in the summer of 1983. He retired from the game a year later but when Bangor City qualified for Europe in 1985, they called on Davies' experience against Fredrikstad and Atletico Madrid, as did Wrexham in the 1985-86 Welsh Cup competition.

DAVIES, GLYN

A Welsh Schoolboy international, Swansea-born Glyn Davies joined Derby County in the summer of 1949. After signing professional forms he had to wait over four years for his league debut which came at Rotherham United in December 1953. Davies was a ferocious tackler and though his skill was limited, he was a tireless leader. Unquestionably committed to the game, he was often accused of playing 'too hard' and was sent off on a number of occasions during his 213 appearances for the Rams.

After failing to agree terms with the then Baseball Ground club, Davies returned to his home-town team where he was made captain. Hampered by injuries he had made just 18 league appearances when he was allowed to leave the Vetch Field and join Yeovil Town as player-manager.

He steered the non-league club to fourth in the Southern League in 1964-65 before returning to manage the Swans at the end of that season. Though Davies said he was committed to attacking football, the Swans' defence leaked goals and ended the campaign in 17th place in the Third Division. The club's sole achievement that campaign was to win the Welsh Cup beating Chester in the final. The club continued to struggle the following season and in October 1966, Davies was sacked.

DAVIES, REG

Born at Cymmer near Swansea and a travelling choirboy in his schooldays, Reg Davies was playing for Southampton at the end of the Second World War. In 1949 after a spell in the army, he joined Southend United but in April 1951 after he had scored 18 goals in 41 league games for the Roots Hall club, Newcastle United paid £9,000 for his services.

He scored on his debut against Wolverhampton Wanderers in a 3-1 win the following October and though he was capped for Wales six times whilst on Tyneside, he never quite clinched a permanent place in the Magpies side during seven seasons at the club. Competition at St James' Park in the 1950s was fierce and the little Welshman's best seasons were 1954-55 and 1955-56. Unfortunately he missed the club's 1955 FA Cup Final appearance because of tonsillitis after being named in the side at inside-forward.

He had scored 50 goals in 170 first team games for United when in October 1958 he moved to Swansea in a cash and player exchange deal involving Ivor Allchurch. On 27 December 1958 he scored a hat-trick for the Swans in a 4-4 draw with Derby County. He went on to score 29 goals in 108 league games for the Welsh club before being transferred to Carlisle United just prior to the start of the 1962-63 season. He later played for Merthyr Tydfil before becoming King's Lynn player-manager in 1965.

DAVIES, WILLIE

Signed from Rhymney for ten shillings and sixpence (52p) he played for Swansea in all the forward positions before settling at outside-right. Davies who won 17 full international caps for Wales, won the first against Scotland in February 1924 when he scored in a 2-0 win. With the Vetch Field club in severe financial difficulties, Davies left the Swans in the summer of 1924 to join Cardiff City for just £25.

At Ninian Park he missed just a handful of games before playing in the 1925 FA Cup Final against Sheffield United. A fast, raiding winger, always likely to pop up in a goalscoring position, he found the net 19 times in 98 games for the Bluebirds before joining Notts County. In his last season with Cardiff, a serious chest illness had caused him to miss the club's victorious 1927 FA Cup Final appearance.

After making 71 appearances in two years at Meadow Lane, he joined Tottenham Hotspur, missing only four of the White Hart Lane club's next 105 League and Cup games. With age beginning to creep up on him, he only appeared in 15 games when Spurs won promotion in 1932-33 and at the end of the season he returned to the Vetch Field for a second spell. He went on to score 22 goals in 131 League games for the Swans before finishing his career at Llanelli. In 1938 he took charge of the caretaking department of Pontarddulais schools.

DEACON, HARRY

Sheffield-born inside-forward Harry Deacon began his Football League career with Birmingham City whom he joined from Hallam FC in 1920. After only two league appearances, he and Len Thompson joined the Swans in the summer of 1922.

In only his third season with the club, he won a Third Division (South) Championship medal as the Swans amassed 57 points and lost only eight games. On 8 November 1924 he hit a hat-trick in a 7-0 home win over Brentford. In the game against Norwich City he is reported to have beaten five men when scoring his second goal against the Canaries. Towards the end of that campaign, the Swans travelled to Plymouth Argyle to play their nearest challengers. The Pilgrims were leading 1-0 with just minutes to go when Harry Deacon's free-kick flew into the roof of the net to secure a most important point. Deacon also scored the club's first ever goal in the Second Division when the Swans entertained South Shields, but the Vetch Field side lost 2-1.

In 1928 Deacon was awarded a benefit match against Heart of Midlothian. A crowd of just over 9,000 turned up to pay tribute to this popular player and also see the first Scottish First Division side ever to play at the Vetch. Deacon went on to score 88 goals in 319 games for the Swans, four of them coming in the 5-5 draw with Blackpool at the Vetch Field in 1929.

DEATH

Little winger 'Tich' Evans was the star of the Swansea side during the early part of the 1919-20 season but midway through the campaign he became depressed following the death of his young wife.

On the Thursday prior to the FA Cup qualifying round game against Gillingham, Swansea trainer Ernie Edwards noticed that 'Tich' was missing from their training session although he had earlier been seen at the ground. Jack Nicholas went to look for the player and when he looked under the Main Stand, in a corner near the players' entrance, he discovered the body of 'Tich' Evans. There was a huge gash to the throat, whilst in his hand was clutched a blood-stained razor.

DEBUTS
Only two players in the history of Swansea Football Club have scored hat-tricks on their debut. The first was Ronnie Williams who scored three goals in the win over Notts County on Christmas Day 1929. He was followed by Bob Latchford who netted his goals in the club's first ever Division One game at the Vetch as Leeds United were beaten 5-1 on 29 August 1981.

DEFEATS - FEWEST
During the 1948-49 and 1969-70 seasons the Swans went through the respective 42 and 46 match programmes suffering only seven defeats as they won the Third Division (South) Championship in 1948-49 and promotion to Division Three after finishing third in Division Four in 1969-70.

DEFEATS - MOST
A total of 27 defeats suffered during the 1983-84 season is the worst in the club's history. Not surprisingly they finished 21st in the Second Division and were relegated.

DEFEATS - WORST
Swansea's record league defeat is 8-1, a scoreline inflicted upon them by Fulham on 22 January 1938, and Newcastle United on 2 September 1939. They have also lost 7-0 in the league on three occasions - Tottenham Hotspur in 1932-33; Bristol Rovers in 1954-55 and Workington in 1960-61.

The club's record cup defeat is 8-0. The Swans lost by this scoreline to Liverpool in an FA Cup third round replay on 9 January 1990 and to Monaco in a European Cup Winners' Cup first round second leg tie on 1 October 1991.

DEFENSIVE RECORDS
Swansea's best defensive record was established in 1948-49 when the club won the Third Division (South) Championship. They conceded just 34 goals in that campaign of 42 matches, losing on just seven occasions.

DENOON, JOCK
Goalkeeper 'Jock' Denoon made his Queen's Park Rangers debut against West Ham United in a London Combination match in January 1917 and went on to play in 89 games for the London club.

He joined Swansea in the summer of 1920 just prior to the club's first season in the Football League. He went on to serve the Welsh club for seven seasons and in 1924-25 when the Swans won the Third Division (South) Championship, he was awarded a benefit for his loyalty to the Vetch Field club. During that Championship winning season, he lost his place to Ted Robson the former Sunderland 'keeper but the veteran custodian won his place back with some impressive performances in the club's reserve side.

He went on to make 173 league appearances for the Swans before joining Tredegar at the end of the 1926-27 season.

DISMISSALS

Billy Ball was the first Swansea player to receive his marching orders when he was sent off during the 1913-14 season, albeit for a minor offence!

Colin Webster was sent off in the club's first European Cup Winners' Cup match against Motor Jena. The game which should have been played at the Vetch was played in Austria after the Foreign Office would not let the Swans' East German opponents into the country. The game held at Linz ended all square at 2-2 but the Germans won the second leg in their own country 5-1.

DRAWS

Swansea played their greatest number of drawn league matches in a single season in 1969-70 when 18 of their matches ended all square and their fewest in seasons 1932-33 and 1950-51 when only four of their matches were drawn.

The club's highest scoring draw is 5-5, the scoreline in the Swans' home match against Blackpool on 27 August 1928.

DWYER, NOEL

Dublin-born goalkeeper Noel Dwyer played his early football with Ormeau FC before signing professional forms for Wolverhampton Wanderers. He went on to spend over five years with the Molineux club but in that time he only managed five league appearances. In December 1958 he switched to West Ham United and though he only played in 36 league games for the Upton Park club, he made the first of his 14 international appearances for the Republic of Ireland when he played against Sweden.

Dwyer joined Swansea in the summer of 1960 and made his debut in a 2-1 defeat at Sunderland on the opening day of the 1960-61 season. After only ten games in which the club were firmly rooted to the foot of the Second Division, Dwyer was dropped before returning to share the goalkeeping duties with Johnny King.

In the sixth round of the 1963-64 FA Cup competition, Noel Dwyer played the game of his life to deny Liverpool at Anfield. He made countless saves and even the dependable Ronnie Moran missed a penalty as Swansea won 2-1. Yet in the semi-final, the Irishman conceded a soft goal to gift Preston North End their winner in a 2-1 defeat. Noel Dwyer had played in 140 league games when he left the Vetch Field in January 1965 to join Plymouth Argyle for £7,500.

He rounded off his professional career with Charlton Athletic before pulling out of league football because of injury.

E

EDMONDSON, JOHN

Centre-forward John Edmondson began his Football League career with Leeds City. He had scored six goals in 11 games but when the Yorkshire club became bankrupt, he was auctioned off along with the club's other assets to meet the claims of the creditors.

In October 1919 he joined Sheffield Wednesday but after just seven months with the Hillsborough club he signed for Swansea for a fee of £500.

Edmondson had a very good first season at the Vetch, ending the campaign as the club's top scorer with 20 goals, including a number of spectacular strikes. A loss of form in 1921-22 led to him losing his first team place and though he recovered his form in 1922-23 he was released at the end of the season, having scored 33 goals in 60 games and joined Exeter City.

EDWARDS, CHRIS

Caerphilly-born central defender Chris Edwards joined Swansea in July 1992 under the Youth Training Scheme after being spotted by scout, Cliff Morris. He was given his chance in the Swansea first team in 1994-95 when manager Frank Burrows adopted a triple central defensive formation in away matches. He made his first appearance for the Welsh Under-21 team against Germany in October 1995 and in April 1996 came on as a substitute for the full Welsh international side in the friendly game against Switzerland.

He continued to impress in the heart of the Swansea defence, his form bringing him to the attention of a number of top clubs. He eventually became unsettled at Vetch Field and after having been placed on the transfer list, spent a ten-day trial period with Nottingham Forest. After being included in the Welsh side to play Scotland in a 'B' international, Edwards who had appeared in 134 League and Cup games for the Swans, signed for Forest for a fee of £175,000 on the transfer deadline day in March 1998.

ELECTION TO FOOTBALL LEAGUE
In May 1920 the Football League decided to form a Third Division and though there was an amendment calling for the decision to be deferred, the proposal at the Football League AGM was carried by quite a large majority.

The Swans along with fellow Welsh clubs Merthyr and Newport were admitted to the Third Division and so after just four seasons of competitive professional football, the Vetch Field club became associate members of the Football League.

EMMANUEL, GARY
The son of former Swan, Len Emmanuel, Swansea-born midfielder Gary Emmanuel began his career with Birmingham City, signing apprentice forms in the summer of 1970.

A year later he turned professional and made his debut against Stoke City in January 1975. Though he was perhaps a shade too slow for the top flight, making 78 league appearances in his time at St Andrews, he went on to carve out a reasonable career for himself in the lower divisions.

In December 1978 he joined Bristol Rovers and played in 65 league games before signing for Swindon Town in a player-exchange deal in the summer of 1981. During his stay at the County Ground, he made 111 league appearances for the Robins before joining Newport County. He was beset by injury problems at Somerton Park and after a short spell with Bristol City, he joined his home-town club in August 1985.

He made his debut for the Swans in a 3-0 home win over Stockport County on the opening day of the 1985-86 season and scored his first goal for the club later that campaign in a 1-0 win over Wolves.

A willing worker, always striving to be in the thick of the action, he made 111 league appearances for the Vetch Field club before a back injury forced his retirement from the game.

Gary Emmanuel

EUROPEAN CUP WINNERS' CUP

As winners of the Welsh Cup in 1960-61 the Swans became the first team from Wales to play in the European Cup Winners' Cup. Drawn against Motor Jena from Austria, the team was obliged to play both legs of their tie away from home. After drawing their 'home' leg 2-2 with goals from Reynolds and a Mel Nurse penalty, they lost 5-1 in the return with Reynolds again finding the net for the Swans.

In 1966-67 the club again went out of the competition in the first round, losing 5-1 on aggregate to the Bulgarian side Slovia Sofia after Keith Todd had netted the Swans' goal in a 1-1 first leg draw at the Vetch.

There was then a gap of 15 seasons before the Swans participated again in the Cup Winners' Cup but sadly with the same results. Facing Lokomotiv Leipzig, the Welsh club again went out in the first round, losing 1-0 at home and 2-1 in East Germany with Jeremy Charles scoring the Swans' goal.

The club's best season in Europe was 1982-83. In the preliminary round they beat Sporting Braga of Portugal 3-0 at the Vetch with Charles netting two of the goals and Portuguese defender Cardoso heading past his own 'keeper. Despite losing the second leg 1-0, the Swans progressed to the first round proper where they recorded a record Welsh win in Europe. Facing Maltese side Sliema Wanderers, the Swans ran out winners 12-0 at the Vetch with eight of the goals coming in the last half-hour. The Swans showed their opponents no mercy in the second leg, winning 5-0 in Malta to ensure that the club progressed to the second round for the only time in their history.

In the second round they met Paris St Germain, a side which included former Spurs and Argentine international Ossie Ardiles. In the first leg at the Vetch Field, the Swans, who were without six first team regulars dominated, but though they had lots of possession, they could not break their opponents down. The only goal of the game came when Toko converted one of the few chances to fall to the French team. In the second leg, the Swans went further behind as early as the fourth minute and though they fought back well, Fernandez added a second goal on the night to give the French side victory 3-0 on aggregate. The following season, the Swans went out at the preliminary round stage, losing 2-1 on aggregate to East German side Magdeburg.

In 1989-90, the Swans were paired with Greek side Panathinaikos in the first round. In the first leg in Athens the home side ran out winners 3-2 with Raynor and Salako netting for the Swans. At the Vetch, Andy Melville scored two goals and Robbie James converted a penalty but the Swans could only manage to draw 3-3 and so went out of the competition 6-5 on aggregate.

The club last participated in the European Cup Winners' Cup in 1991-92 when they met Monaco of France. After losing 2-1 at home to the French side with Andrew Legg netting for the Welsh club, the Swans then suffered their heaviest defeat in Europe when they lost 8-0 in Monaco, 10-1 on aggregate!

EVANS, BRIAN

A winger in the old-fashioned mode, Brian Evans joined Swansea from Abergavenny in the summer of 1963 when Trevor Morris paid the Welsh League club just £650 for his services.

Over the next ten seasons, Evans was to give the Vetch Field club great service, missing very few games. Very quick off the mark, he soon won Welsh Under-23 honours and in 1972 won the first of seven caps at full international level when he played for Wales against Finland. Just prior to that, he, along with goalkeeper Tony Millington and Dave Gwyther, was selected to tour New Zealand with an FA of Wales party.

Evans went on to score 58 goals in 355 league appearances before Swansea manager Harry Gregg felt obliged to sell him to Hereford United for a fee of £7,000 as he had to off-load before he could buy.

The flying winger scored nine goals in 48 league games for the Edgar Street club before leaving to play non-league football. He now runs a successful painting and decorating business in Swansea.

EVANS, IAN

Ian Evans began his league career with Queen's Park Rangers and was with the Loftus Road club when they won promotion to the First Division in 1972-73. He then joined Crystal Palace in an exchange deal which took Don Rogers to Loftus Road in September 1974.

Evans was an ever-present in the Palace side that won promotion from the Third Division in 1976-77 and his form was such that he broke into the full Welsh side, winning 13 caps. After breaking his leg in a challenge with George Best, Evans failed to regain his first team place, despite returning to full fitness. He signed for Barnsley for £80,000 after a spell on loan and helped the Oakwell club win promotion to the Second Division. After spells on loan to Exeter City and Cambridge United, he became coach at Selhurst Park before becoming manager of Swansea in February 1989.

At the end of his first season the club were placed 12th in the Third Division but in 1989 90 he had more of a difficult time at Vetch Field and after only a year in charge, he was sacked.

EVANS, ROY

At the end of the 1962-63 season, his first at the Vetch Field, full-back Roy Evans played for the Welsh Under-23s, later making two more appearances at that level. He was a virtual ever-present in the Swansea side for the next few seasons and when Vic Gomersall joined the Swans from Manchester City, the two formed one of the club's best full-back pairings since the Second World War.

Evans won one full cap for Wales when he played against Northern Ireland at Ninian Park in 1964, a match the Welsh lost 3-2.

He went on to appear in 213 league games, scoring eight goals before leaving the Vetch in 1967 to join Hereford United. Both he and Brian Purcell were tragically killed in a car crash in 1969.

EVANS, WYNDHAM

After playing his early football in the Carmarthenshire League Wyndham Evans became briefly connected with Stoke City and played for the club as an amateur.

Swansea manager Roy Bentley invited him to play for a Swansea Combination side and then Evans played in the Reserves as part-time professional under the guidance of team manager Roy Saunders.

He made his first team debut for the Swans against Bristol Rovers during the 1969-70 season and the following campaign signed as a full-time professional. In 1973-74, Evans was appointed as the club's captain and was an inspiration to all who played under him. The Llanelli-born full-back was a member of the Swansea team that won promotion from the Fourth Division to the First in four seasons.

In the club's first season in the top flight, he made his First Division against Tottenham Hotspur, later realising an ambition when he played against Manchester United, his 350th league appearance.

The long-serving Evans who was granted a testimonial match against Liverpool, stayed with the Swans as a player until 1982 but returned as player-coach under John Toshack before finally bowing out of the game in 1985 after playing in 391 league matches.

F

FA CUP

Swansea first entered the FA Cup in 1913-14 and after winning through five qualifying rounds, became the first Welsh club to reach the first round proper where they beat Merthyr 2-0. Despite being drawn at home again in the second round, the Swans lost 2-1 to Queen's Park Rangers.

In 1914-15 the Swans were drawn at home to play Blackburn Rovers who were the current League Champions having finished seven points clear of runners-up Aston Villa. In fact in the season that they played Swansea, they finished third in Division One, only three points adrift of champions Everton. Despite constant pressure from the Lancashire club, it was Ben Beynon who scored the only goal of the first half to give Swansea the lead. In the second-half, Rovers were awarded a penalty, but Bradshaw who had scored from 36 consecutive spot-kicks hit his shot wide. After that the Swans defended in depth and hung on to cause one of the biggest upsets in the game of football up to that time. Sadly, the Swans' success was shortlived. In the next round they went out to Newcastle United, losing 2-0 at home after the first match at St James' Park ended all square at 1-1.

In 1925-26, the Swans' first ever campaign in Division Two, they reached the semi-finals of the FA Cup for the first time in their history. In the first round, goals from Thompson, Nicholas and Deacon gave the Swans a 3-1 victory at Exeter City and a home tie against Watford in round two. In an exciting match, the Swans won 3-2 despite missing a penalty.

Blackpool were Swansea's opponents in round three, but in a hard fought game at Bloomfield Road, Jock Denoon was in fine form and Fowler and Deacon scored the goals that gave the club a 2-0 win. The fourth round paired Swansea with Stoke, a club that they had played twice over Christmas and drawn 1-1 on both occasions. This time Jack Fowler netted four goals in a 6-3 win for the Swans.

The Vetch side travelled to Millwall for the fifth round where the goalscoring hero of the previous tie, Jack Fowler scored the game's only goal three minutes from time. In the sixth round, Swansea were drawn at home to the mighty Arsenal. The Welsh side took the lead on the stroke of half-time when Len Thompson, who was later to join the Gunners beat his man and shot high into the roof of the net. After Fowler had added a second early in the second-half, Denoon let a long-range effort from an Arsenal player slip through his hands to put the London club back in the game. Despite the whole of the Swansea team being penned in their own half for the rest of the game, they hung on for a memorable victory. In the semi-final, Swansea met Bolton Wanderers at White Hart Lane, but experience told and the Lancashire club won 3-0.

The following season when Cardiff won the Cup, Swansea reached the quarter-finals and had they not lost 3-1 to Reading, would have met the Bluebirds in the semi-finals.

In 1933-34, the Swans progressed to the fifth round beating Notts County (Home 1-0) and Bury (Home 3-0 after a 1-1 draw at Gigg Lane) before losing to the only goal of the game at First Division Portsmouth.

The club reached the fifth round stage again in 1936-37 with victories over Carlisle United (Home 1-0) and York City (Away 3-1 after a goalless draw at the Vetch) before going down 3-0 at Sunderland.

The Swans were to reach the fifth round stage twice in the 1950s. In 1951-52, the Swans won 3-0 at Reading and then defeated Rotherham at the Vetch by the same scoreline. In the fifth round, they entertained Newcastle United who were riding high in the First Division and though the Swans played exceptionally well, they lost 1-0. In 1954-55 the Welsh side won 2-0 at Blackburn Rovers and then defeated Stoke 2-1 in front of a Vetch Field crowd of 27,892 before losing 1-0 at Sunderland after the first game in South Wales had finished all-square at 2-2.

In 1963-64 the Swans reached the semi-final of the FA Cup for the second time in their history. In the third round, goals from Brian Evans, Herbie Williams, Roy Evans and Eddie Thomas helped them beat Barrow 4-1. In the next round, Swansea visited Bramall Lane to play Sheffield United.

The Welsh side were very much the underdogs but another Eddie Thomas goal gave them a 1-1 draw and took the tie to a replay at the Vetch where the Swans won 4-0 with young Derek Draper scoring two of the goals. The fifth round brought another difficult draw, away to Stoke City but thanks to two goals by Keith Todd, who was deputising for the injured Eddie Thomas, the Swans gained a 2-2 draw and another replay at the Vetch. Todd was on target again, as was McLaughlin and the Welsh side were through to the sixth round where they were drawn to play Liverpool at Anfield. The Merseysiders who were to win that season's League Championship were rocked when the Swans scored two goals in the space of four minutes towards the end of the first-half. Jimmy McLaughlin had shot the Swans ahead in the 37th minute and then the Irish winger set up a second for Eddie Thomas. Peter Thompson reduced Swansea's lead on the hour but then Republic of Ireland international 'keeper Noel Dwyer produced a series of breathtaking saves to deny the Liverpool forwards. When Ronnie Moran failed with a penalty attempt, Swansea were through to the semi-finals. After taking a first-half lead against Preston North End at Villa Park, two second-half goals from Alex Dawson and Tony Singleton ended the Swans' dreams.

The following season the club reached the fifth round for the eighth time, only to lose 2-0 at home to Peterborough United after the first game at London Road had been goalless.

In 1966-67 the Swans recorded their highest score in the FA Cup when they beat non-league Folkestone 7-2 after the first game had been drawn 2-2. The club's heaviest defeat in the competition came in 1989-90 when Liverpool, who were held to a goalless draw at the Vetch, gained revenge for that 1963-64 upset with a resounding 8-0 win at Anfield.

The Swans last reached the fifth round of the FA Cup in 1979-80 where they lost 2-0 at West Ham United. In 1998-99 Swansea beat the Hammers 1-0 at the Vetch after a 1-1 draw at Upton Park before going out 1-0 in the fourth round to another Premier League club, Derby County.

FASTEST RISE

Swansea went from the Fourth Division to the First in the fastest time in Football League history. Since the creation of the Fourth Division in 1958, only Northampton Town had gone from Fourth to First but it took them four years to make the journey. The Swans did it in three years, winning promotion from the Fourth Division at the end of the 1977-78 season along with Watford, Southend United and Brentford. The following season they went straight through the Third Division, going up behind Shrewsbury Town and Watford.

After two seasons in the Second Division, the club achieved the greatest promotion of them all behind West Ham United and Notts County. In just over three years, manager John Toshack had done the impossible.

Season	Division	P	W	D	L	F	A	Pts	Position
1977-78	4	46	23	10	13	87	47	56	3rd
1978-79	3	46	24	12	10	83	61	60	3rd
1979-80	2	42	17	9	16	48	53	43	12th
1980-81	2	42	18	14	10	64	44	50	3rd

FATHER AND SON

Swansea have boasted a number of father and son players. Billy Hole was a member of the Swansea side in the 1920s, scoring 40 goals in 341 league games for the club. He won nine international caps and was a member of the Vetch Field side that won promotion to the Second Division for the first time in the club's history in 1924-25. Three of his sons, Colin, Alan and Barrie all played for Swansea. Colin, a Welsh Schoolboy international appeared in just one league game whilst Alan made 20 appearances in that same Second Division season of 1953-54. Barrie Hole joined the Swans from Aston Villa when the Welsh side were in the Third Division. The winner of 30 Welsh caps, he appeared in 78 league games for the Vetch Field club.

Ivor Jones was another outstanding Swansea player of the 1920s. His sons Bryn and Cliff also played for the Welsh club. Bryn made 121 league appearances for the Swans, later playing for Newport County, Bournemouth, Northampton Town and Watford. Cliff who scored 47 goals in 168 league games for the Vetch Field side joined Spurs for £35,000 in February 1958, a record fee for a winger. A member of the White Hart Lane club's double-winning side of 1960-61, he scored 159 goals in 378 games for Spurs as well as winning 59 caps for Wales.

Sid Lawrence, a Welsh international who won eight caps for his country and made 312 league appearances for the Swans was one of the club's star defenders. His son David who played full-back for the Vetch Field club in the sixties, appeared in 97 league games.

Len Emmanuel lost much of his career to the Second World War, only appearing in four league games before joining Newport County. His son Gary who won honours for his country at Under-23 level, started his career at Birmingham City, but after spells at Bristol Rovers, Swindon Town, Newport County and Bristol City, he arrived at the Vetch Field to play in 111 league games for the Swans.

Mel Charles, brother of the legendary John, appeared in 233 games, scoring 69 goals before going on to play for Arsenal. His son Jeremy played for the Swans in the 1980s and was in the side that won promotion to Division One for the first time in the club's history.

Dean Saunders who went on to win fame with Liverpool, Aston Villa and Wales scored 12 goals in 49 games for Swansea whilst his father Roy played 95 games at wing-half following his transfer from Liverpool.

FEENEY, JIM

Classical full-back Jim Feeney joined Swansea from Linfield in December 1946 and over the next four seasons made 88 appearances for the Vetch Field club. He won a Third Division (South) Championship medal in 1948-49 but in March 1950 he joined Ipswich Town with fellow Irish international Sam McCrory for a combined fee of £10,500.

Feeney made his Ipswich debut in the East Anglian derby at Carrow Road just a few days after joining the club and was a virtual ever-present for the next six seasons. In 1953-54 he missed just two matches as the Portman Road club won the Third Division (South) Championship and the following season was outstanding in the Ipswich defence even though they were relegated from the Second Division.

He played the last of his 232 League and Cup games at Brighton in September 1956. In that game he suffered a broken nose in the sixth minute, reducing the side to ten men!

FERGUSON, ALEX

Goalkeeper Alex Ferguson began his career with Gillingham where his impressive performances alerted the Swansea board, and in February 1927 he joined the Vetch Field club, primarily as cover for the long-serving Jock Denoon.

However, the young 'keeper's performances in the Swansea Reserve side led to him displacing the experienced Denoon, who was allowed to leave the Vetch at the end of the 1926-27 season. In his first season with the Swans, Ferguson turned in a number of outstanding displays as the Welsh side finished the campaign in sixth place in the Second Division.

Between 29 September 1928 and 7 March 1931, Ferguson appeared in 108 consecutive league games - a club record at that time.

One of the club's greatest goalkeepers, he went on to appear in 270 league games before being made available for transfer at the end of the 1935-36 season.

FIRST DIVISION
Following their meteoric rise to the First Division, Swansea's only spell in the top flight lasted just two seasons.

On 29 August 1981, the club beat Leeds United 5-1 with Bob Latchford scoring a hat-trick in what was the Swans' first match in Division One. In the club's first season in the top flight, they topped the First Division table on three separate occasions, and in the New Year produced a nine-match unbeaten run that made them serious Championship contenders. However, after losing five of their last six matches, the Swans had to be content with sixth place.

After a goalless draw at Notts County on the opening day of the 1982-83 season, the Swans beat Coventry and Norwich before four successive defeats set the tone for the season. Because the club were behind in their payments for the £150,000 they had spent on Everton's Garry Stanley, the Football League banned them from buying new players and so they could not strengthen the side.

The Swans turned to youngsters but sadly they did not have the knowledge or experience to keep the club in the top flight.

FIRST LEAGUE MATCH
Swansea's first league match was played at Fratton Park on 28 August 1920 against Portsmouth. A crowd of 20,232 saw the Swans lose 3-0 to goals from Stringfellow, James and Reid. The Swansea side on that historic day was: J.Crumley; F.E.Robson; W.B.Evans; F.Smith; J.Holdsworth; J.L.Williams; B.Hole; I.Jones; J.Edmondson; H.Rigsby and J.Spottiswood.

FIRST MATCH
The club's first competitive game was a Southern League fixture played against Cardiff at the Vetch Field in September 1912. The game ended all square at 1-1 with Billy Ball netting for the Swans.

FLOODLIGHTS
Swansea played their first match under floodlights at Cheltenham during the 1952-53 season, though floodlights at the Vetch Field were not installed until the beginning of the 1960-61 campaign. They were officially opened on 10

October 1960 when the Swans met opposition in Heart of Midlothian in a friendly. For the record, the match ended all square at 4-4.

In 1977 the club installed new floodlights, and the match against Bradford City on St David's Day was chosen to inaugurate them. In that game the Swans lost 3-2.

FOOTBALL LEAGUE CUP

Swansea have made little impact on the Football League Cup. (later Milk, Littlewoods, Rumbelows, Coca Cola and Worthington Cup)

Since the commencement of the competition the Vetch Field club have never made it past the fourth round. That stage was first reached in 1964-65 when they entered the Cup at the second round stage and beat Swindon Town 3-1 at home.

In the third round, the Swans travelled to Millmoor and drew 2-2 with Rotherham United before winning the replay at the Vetch 2-0. For the next round, Swansea had to travel to Stamford Bridge to play First Division Chelsea and though they put up a tremendous fight, they lost 3-2 to that season's eventual winners.

The Swans reached the fourth round stage of the League Cup again in 1976-77. In the first round they beat Newport County 4-2 on aggregate and then defeated Chester at Sealand Road 3-2 before winning a third round tie at Torquay United 2-1. In the fourth round, the Swans entertained Bolton Wanderers but were held to a 1-1 draw before crashing out of the competition 5-1 in the replay at Burnden Park.

The Swans lost their first ever match in the League Cup 2-1 at home to Blackburn Rovers before losing 6-5 on aggregate to Ipswich Town in 1961-62, the first of a number of high-scoring League Cup matches played over two legs. In fact, the Swans didn't win a League Cup tie until 25 September 1963 when they beat Sunderland 3-1 at the Vetch.

The club's best victory in the League Cup came in the 1978-79 season when they beat Newport County 5-0 in the second leg of that first round tie to win 6-2 on aggregate with Robbie James netting a hat-trick. The only other players to score a hat-trick for the Swans in the League Cup are Alan Waddle and Bob Latchford. Alan Waddle's hat-trick came in the 4-1 home win over Bournemouth in 1979-80, whilst Bob Latchford's three goals were scored in the 3-0 defeat of Bristol Rovers in 1982-83.

Swansea have saved two of their best performances in the League Cup for Tottenham Hotspur. In 1978-79, the Welsh club were held to a 2-2 draw at the Vetch in front of 24,335 fans before goals from Charles, Curtis and

Toshack gave them a 3-1 win in the replay at White Hart Lane. In 1991-92, Swansea beat the London club 1-0 at the Vetch, courtesy of a Jimmy Gilligan goal, but were heavily beaten 5-1 in the second leg with substitute Shaun Chapple netting for the Swans.

FORD, JON

A versatile player, Birmingham-born Jon Ford began his league career with Swansea after joining the Vetch Field club from Cradley Heath for a fee of £5,000 in the summer of 1991.

He soon established himself as a first team regular at Swansea and missed very few games in four seasons with the Welsh club. He had appeared in 206 first team games for the Swans when he was transferred to Bradford City for £210,000 in July 1995.

After playing his early football in midfield, Ford became a strong and determined centre-half, though he could also play at left-back. His time at Valley Parade was hampered by having to undergo two separate operations on his right knee, and after just one season he left to join Gillingham. His stay at the Priestfield Stadium lasted just six months during which time he made only six first team appearances before moving to Barnet for £25,000.

He was soon appointed club captain and has proved himself a valuable asset during his time at Underhill.

FORD, TREVOR

As a youngster, Trevor Ford was encouraged in his football by his father and played for Swansea Schoolboys as a full-back, only missing his Welsh cap due to a broken leg. He was also a very talented cricketer but after trials with a number of clubs, he set his sights on a career in football.

During the Second World War, Ford served in the Royal Artillery and as the Service Team already had two full-backs he was tried at centre-forward. He graduated into the Swansea first team during the latter stages of the war, having signed for them in 1942. In the 1945-46 season, he hit the headlines by scoring 41 goals and gained a place in the Welsh side for the last Victory international of the campaign against Northern Ireland at Ninian Park. He had scored nine goals in 16 league games for Swansea in the 1946-47 season when Aston Villa won the race to sign one of the hottest properties in the game.

Whilst with Villa, Ford turned down offers from Colombia and Portugal but in 1950 he joined Sunderland for a then record fee of £30,000. However, he failed to settle at Roker Park and in 1953 returned to South

Wales with Cardiff City. At international level he soon became the leading goalscorer of all-time and in 38 games scored 23 goals including a hat-trick against Belgium.

He wrote a book which lifted the lid off illegal payments to players in the Football League. When it was serialised in a Sunday newspaper he found himself suspended. Though he won his case for reinstatement he was soon suspended again when he was named along with other Sunderland players as having accepted such payments during his stay with the Wearsiders.

He then went to play for PSV Eindhoven in Holland for three years until the ban was lifted, after which he joined Newport County before ending his career with non-league Romford.

FORMATION

In 1900 former schoolboy players got together to form the Swansea and District League and by 1909, the interest in soccer had grown to such an extent that it was decided to form a senior club in the town.

One of the main obstacles was the availability of a central ground but all was resolved in 1912 when the Swansea Gaslight Company failed to get Parliamentary permission to develop the Vetch Field site after strong opposition from the residents of Sandfields.

There was a lot of enthusiasm for the game of soccer and on 14 June 1912, a meeting was held at the Royal Hotel and the new club was formed. The first chairman was Mr J.W.Thorpe, a Swansea solicitor and clerk to Pontardawe Justices and the first secretary was Mr S.B.Williams.

Armed with a seven year lease, the Welsh club went about preparing the team with goalkeeper Walter Whittaker the first manager.

FOURTH DIVISION

Swansea have had three spells in the Fourth Division. Their first from 1967-68 lasted three seasons until 1969-70 when the club finished third and won promotion to Division Three. The Swans lasted just three seasons in the Third Division before relegation in 1972-73 saw them return to the league's basement for a second spell. This time the Welsh club spent five seasons in the Fourth Division, having to apply for re-election to the league for the only time in their history in 1974-75 when they ended the season in 22nd place. They won promotion in 1977-78 when they again finished third in the league with 56 points.

That was the start of the Swans winning promotion three times in four

59

seasons, culminating in them playing two seasons in the top flight. The reverse happened when the Vetch Field club were relegated three times in four seasons, beginning their last spell in the Fourth Division in 1986-87. The following season the club finished sixth in Division Four but won promotion via the play-offs.

FOWLER, JACK

Jack Fowler joined Swansea from Plymouth Argyle in March 1924 for a fee of £1,280 and made a goalscoring debut in the home match against Southend United. The following month he scored the first of nine hat-tricks for the club against Brentford.

He scored both goals in the club's 2-0 home win over Swindon Town on the opening day of the 1924-25 season and then netted another double against Merthyr Town in the next match. When the Swans played Charlton Athletic on 27 September 1924, Fowler set an individual scoring record for a league match when he hit five of the club's goals in a 6-1 win. He netted another hat-trick in November as Luton Town were beaten at the Vetch. In February 1925 Fowler won the first of six Welsh caps when he played against England at Swansea.

The Swans who won the Third Division (South) Championship that season had Fowler to thank for scoring the opening goal, his 28th of the season, in the final match against Exeter City which they had to win to secure the title - Len Thompson added a second in a 2-1 win.

Fowler's fourth hat-trick for the club came on Christmas Day 1925 at Darlington, quickly followed by another treble against Preston North End in January 1926. At the end of that month, the Swans beat Stoke 6-3 in the fourth round of the FA Cup and Fowler who was in superb form, netted four of them. He scored another hat-trick that season, as Southampton were well beaten at the Vetch and netted Swansea's second goal in the 2-1 FA Cup quarter-final victory over Arsenal but sadly he couldn't repeat the feat in the semi-final against Bolton Wanderers.

In 1926-27 the club raced to the top of the table and were unbeaten in their opening seven games. On 8 September 1926, Fowler scored his seventh hat-trick in a 5-2 win over Barnsley and three weeks later hit another against Darlington. His last hat-trick came in a 6-0 win over Wolves the following season and in the match against Tottenham Hotspur on 10 November 1928 he netted his 100th and last league goal for the club in a 4-0 win.

An idol of the Swansea crowd, Jack Fowler rarely missed an opportunity to shoot, scoring his 100 league goals in just 176 games.

FREESTONE, ROGER

Goalkeeper Roger Freestone joined his home-town team Newport County as a trainee in 1986 but within nine months he had moved to Chelsea for a fee of £95,000. An excellent shot-stopper, he went on to appear in 53 games for the Stamford Bridge club when, after loan spells with Swansea and Hereford United he joined the Swans on a permanent basis in September 1991.

One of the club's most consistent 'keepers, he did not miss a single league game until April 1995 when he was called up to to Welsh international squad for the match against Germany. In 1995-96 he converted a couple of penalties for the Swans during the first month of the season and missed just one game.

One of the best 'keepers outside the Premier League, his consistency for the Swans has been a major factor in the club reaching the play-offs on three occasions and winning the Autoglass Trophy. Freestone who signed a new four year contract in the summer of 1997 has appeared in over 450 first team games for the club.

Roger Freestone

FREIGHT ROVER TROPHY

A competition designed solely and specifically for the Associate Members of the Football league, the Freight Rover Trophy replaced the initial Associate Members Cup for the 1984-85 season.

After beating Bristol Rovers 2-0 at the Vetch in a first round first leg tie, the Swans travelled to Eastville and after playing out a goalless draw won through to the knockout stages of the competition. Drawn away to Newport County, the Swans again kept a blank sheet but also having failed to score themselves, won through to the third round on penalties. They were then beaten 2-0 at home by Brentford who went all the way to Wembley only to lose to Wigan Athletic in the final.

In 1985-86, the Swans were grouped with Cardiff City and Newport County, winning 2-0 and drawing 1-1 respectively to qualify for the knockout stages. After beating Torquay United 1-0, the Swans drew 0-0 at Hereford United in the Southern Area semi-final before losing on penalties.

In 1986-87, the Swans drew their opening group game 0-0 at Torquay United before beating Walsall 3-0 at the Vetch. In the next round however, they went crashing out of the tournament after losing 2-0 at Aldershot.

G

GILLIGAN, JIMMY

Former England Youth international Jimmy Gilligan began his Football League career with Watford but in almost six years at Vicarage Road, the bustling centre-forward made just 27 league appearances in which he scored six goals. After a loan spell with Lincoln City, he joined Grimsby Town for a fee of £100,000, but he couldn't settle at Blundell Park and was transferred to Swindon Town. He was soon on the move again, this time to Lincoln City after a loan spell with Newport County.

When the Imps lost their Football League status in 1987, Gilligan joined Cardiff City for what proved to be a bargain fee of £17,500. After scoring on his debut, he ended his first season at Ninian Park as the Bluebirds' leading scorer with 20 goals as the club won promotion to the Third Division. He top scored again the following season and netted a hat-trick in a 4-0 home win over Derry City in the European Cup Winners' Cup. During the early part of the 1989-90 season, he followed former Bluebirds manager Frank Burrows to Portsmouth before returning to South Wales to end his league career with Swansea.

He made his league debut for the Swans in a 3-0 defeat at Leyton Orient on the opening day of the 1990-91 season, a campaign in which he was the club's top scorer with 16 league goals including a hat-trick in a 4-2 win at Wigan Athletic and eight goals in other competitions. A model professional, he played through the majority of those games with a painful back condition. He netted his second hat-trick for the club in a 3-0 home win over Chester City in 1991-92 after making a good recovery from microsurgery on his back.

GOALKEEPERS

Swansea has almost always been extremely well served by its goalkeepers and most of them have been highly popular with the supporters.

The club's first notable goalkeeper was player-manager Walter Whittaker who had begun his career with Blackburn Rovers before joining Exeter City. Signing for Swansea in 1912, he performed effectively between the posts in the club's first professional season.

Jock Denoon joined Swansea in the summer of 1920 and was the club's 'keeper during their first season in the Football League. He went on to make 173 league appearances for the Welsh club, winning a Third Division (South) League Championship medal in 1924-25.

Alex Ferguson joined the club as cover for Denoon but his performances in the Swans' Reserve side soon led to him displacing the experienced Denoon. He went on to establish a club record, since equalled by Andrew Legg, of 108 consecutive league appearances.

John King who played his first game for the Swans in 1950 holds the club league appearance record for a goalkeeper having played in 368 games. In 14 seasons at the Vetch, King was a virtual ever-present until he was replaced by Noel Dwyer in 1964. The Republic of Ireland international 'keeper was outstanding in the club's run to the FA Cup semi-finals, playing the game of his life in the Swans' 2-1 sixth round success at Liverpool.

Welsh international goalkeeper Tony Millington helped the club win promotion to the Third Division in 1969-70, keeping 20 clean sheets and in 1971-72 equalled Jack Parry's record sequence of being unbeaten in five consecutive games. That record was later broken by Dai Davies who appeared in 77 league games for the Swans.

Jimmy Rimmer was initially loaned to Swansea in October 1973 from manager Harry Gregg's old club, Manchester United. He later found fame with Arsenal and Aston Villa, where he won international recognition and League Championship, European Cup and European Super Cup medals. He signed for Swansea on a permanent basis in the summer of 1983 before later becoming the club's Youth team coach.

The club's present 'keeper is Roger Freestone, who has proved himself to be one of the best outside the Premier League. His consistency has taken him to 369 league appearances up to the end of the 1998-99 season passing John King's club record of 368 games.

GOALS

The most goals Swansea have ever scored in one game is their 12-0 victory against Maltese side Sliema Wanderers in a first round European Cup Winners' Cup tie on 1 September 1982. Substitute Ian Walsh scored a hat-trick, Jeremy Charles and Jim Loveridge scored two goals apiece and one each from Bob Latchford, Nigel Stevenson, Dzemal Hadziabdic, Colin Irwin and Ante Rajkovic.

GOALS - CAREER BEST

The highest goalscorer in the club's history is Ivor Allchurch who, between 1949 to 1958 and 1965 to 1968, netted 189 goals for the club. These comprised of 166 in the League, nine in the FA Cup, four in the Football League Cup and ten in the Welsh Cup.

GOALS - INDIVIDUAL

The only player to score five goals in a Football League match for Swansea is Jack Fowler who achieved the feat in a Third Division (South) game against Charlton Athletic at the Vetch Field on 27 September 1924. For the record, Swansea won 6-1.

GOALS - SEASON

The club's highest League goalscorer in any one season remains Cyril Pearce who scored 35 league goals as Swansea finished 15th in the Second Division in 1931-32. The season's highest tally for all matches is the 39 goals achieved by Pearce during the same season when he netted four goals in the Welsh Cup, a competition the Swans won by beating Wrexham in the final.

GOMERSALL, VIC

Left-back Vic Gomersall began his Football League career with his hometown club, Manchester City and, after working his way up through the ranks, played his first game during the 1960-61 season. For much of his six seasons at Maine Road, Gomersall found himself as Glyn Pardoe's understudy and when he left to join Swansea in August 1966 he had only appeared in 39 league games.

Very strong in the tackle and a tireless worker, Gomersall was a very reliable defender. He soon established himself in the Swansea side and formed an outstanding full-back partnership with Roy Evans. In 1967-68, and only his second season with the club, he was voted the club's Player of the Year. In 1969-70 he helped the Swans win promotion to the Third Division. At the end of the following season, Gomersall, who had scored six goals in 180 league games left the Vetch to play non-league football.

GREEN, HAYDN

Haydn Green was appointed Swansea's manager in June 1939 having previously had managerial experience with Lincoln City and Hull City, whom he took to the Third Division (North) Championship in 1932-33. He had been in charge of Southern League Guildford City whom he led to the Championship in 1937-38 immediately before arriving at the Vetch Field.

He was confident that he would be successful at the Welsh club when the outbreak of the Second World War interrupted his planning. During the war years, Green adopted the title of secretary-manager but struggled to find players. One year he gave up his Christmas dinner to sign Trevor Ford, arriving back home for his dinner after midnight! As well as instigating a youth policy, he suggested significant ground improvements, though due to financial constraints, his only real innovation was the installation of a broadcasting system.

When league football resumed in 1946-47, Green proved himself to be astute in the transfer market, going to Ireland to sign players of the calibre of Sam McCrory, Norman Lockhart, Jim Feeney, Rory Keane and Jack O'Driscoll, all of whom were to gain international recognition.

Green resigned in September 1947 following a failed bid for England centre-forward Tommy Lawton. He later managed Watford but had little success in his 14 months in charge.

GREGG, HARRY

Harry Gregg began his footballing career with Dundalk and was a part-timer with Coleraine when he was snapped up by Doncaster Rovers in the summer of 1951. He had made 93 league appearances for the Belle Vue club when Matt Busby signed him for Manchester United in December 1957 for what was then a record fee for a goalkeeper of £23,000.

His form was such that United won a place in the European Cup semi-finals following a 3-3 draw against Red Star in Belgrade. The plane that was carrying home the United team crashed on the runway at Munich Airport, killing many of the players. Harry Gregg crawled virtually unscathed from the wreckage, and as the plane's crew shouted for people to get away from the aircraft for fear of fire, he returned to the plane and helped some of the passengers to safety.

Three months later he kept goal in the 1958 FA Cup Final which

United lost 2-0 to Bolton Wanderers, being shoulder barged into the net by Nat Lofthouse for the Trotters' second goal.

Despite his disappointments at Wembley, Gregg had a superb year at international level as Northern Ireland qualified for the World Cup Finals. Gregg continued his superb displays for United and Northern Ireland, for whom he won 25 caps until December 1966 when he joined Stoke City.

A shoulder injury limited his appearances at the Victoria Ground and he entered management with Shrewsbury Town, whom he steered away from relegation in 1968-69. He became Swansea manager in November 1972 but was unable to prevent their relegation to the Fourth Division at the end of the season.

Gregg went back to Old Trafford and persuaded Manchester United to allow goalkeeper Jimmy Rimmer to play for the Swans on a loan basis. He also unearthed some fine young players but as soon as they began to show some potential, they were sold. In January 1975, Gregg resigned from his post at the Vetch for this reason and out of sheer frustration. After a spell in charge at Crewe, he returned to the Vetch Field as coach. In July 1984 he was appointed assistant to Lou Macari but departed in April 1985 after the two former Manchester United stars ended up not speaking to each other!

GRIFFITHS, HARRY

One of the club's most popular and loyal servants, Harry Griffiths represented Swansea Schoolboys in their first season directly after the Second World War. He joined Swansea's groundstaff at the age of 15 and signed professional forms two years later.

He made his Football League debut against Chesterfield in 1948-49 at outside-right and after establishing himself as a first team regular in 1951-52, rarely missed a game in the next 11 seasons.

Griffiths was one of the club's greatest utility players, appearing in every position in the Swansea side except centre-half and goalkeeper. He won one full cap for Wales when he played against Northern Ireland at Windsor Park, Belfast in April 1953 in a match the Welsh side won 3-2. He left the club in 1964 after scoring 68 goals in 424 league games including hat-tricks against Leicester City in March 1956 and Doncaster Rovers in October 1956.

He became player-manager at Merthyr and remained there for two seasons before returning to Swansea as the club's first team trainer under former manager Billy Lucas. Griffiths was appointed the Swans manager in January 1975 and almost led the club to promotion from the Fourth Division in 1976-77, missing out by just one point after a fine run-in. He left the club through ill-health before the Swans went up the following season.

He had returned to help the club out when he died at the early age of 47 whilst working in the treatment room at Vetch Field prior to Swansea's match against Scunthorpe United on 25 April 1978, a match the Welsh club won 3-1.

GUEST PLAYERS

The 'guest' system was used by all clubs during the two wars. Although at times it was abused almost beyond belief (in that some sides that opposed Swansea had ten or 11 'guests'!) it normally worked sensibly and effectively to the benefit of players, clubs and supporters alike.

The most distinguished players to 'guest' for Swansea were Welsh international Leslie Jones who was with Arsenal and Ernie Jones who was on Bolton Wanderers' books. Both players returned to the Vetch Field on a permanent basis after the Second World War. Other players to 'guest' for the club included Norman Corbett (West Ham United), Jack Hodgson (Grimsby Town) Len Stansbridge (Southampton) and Cyril Trigg (Birmingham City).

GWYTHER, DAVE

Dave Gwyther joined Swansea from South Gower in March 1966 and over the next eight seasons proved himself a more than useful goalscorer. The Birmingham-born forward first showed his potential in 1968-69 when he finished second in the club's scoring charts to Herbie Williams. His ability to find the back of the net led to Bristol Rovers offering £8,000 for his services. Thankfully Swansea did not accept their offer.

On 6 December 1969, his 21st birthday, he scored four goals for Swansea, all headed against Oxford City in an FA Cup second round tie. In 1970-71, Gwyther was not only Swansea's leading scorer but also the top scorer in Division Three. Included in this total was his only league hat-trick for the club in a 5-0 win over Reading on 27 March 1971. His reward at the end of that campaign was election for the FA of Wales party to tour New Zealand in the close season. The club continued to refuse all offers for Gwyther, notably a £20,000 bid from Cardiff City.

Gwyther, who was capped twice by Wales at Under-23 level left Vetch Field in the summer of 1973 after having scored 59 goals in 217 league games to join Halifax Town for £12,000. He later played for Rotherham United, Newport County and Crewe Alexandra before leaving to play non-league football with Port Talbot Athletic.

H

HANFORD, HARRY

Swansea-born Harry Hanford was a member of the Vetch Field club's groundstaff and made his first team debut towards the end of the 1927-28 season. Over the next few seasons, Hanford's form was such that a number of top flight clubs showed an interest in him. But despite a couple of firm offers, the popular Hanford remained at the Vetch Field.

By the early 1930s, Hanford had become a very effective centre-half and was captaining the club. In 1934 he won the first of three full caps for Wales whilst with Swansea when he played against Northern Ireland but midway through the 1935-36 season, Hanford, who had played in 200 league games for the Swans joined Sheffield Wednesday for a substantial fee.

At Hillsborough he won a further four caps for his country and appeared in 94 games for the Owls before moving to Exeter City where he ended his league career.

HARRIS, MARK

Defender Mark Harris was a late entrant into League football signing for Crystal Palace in 1988 at the age of 24 from Wokingham Town of the Vauxhall Opel League. After two games as substitute in Palace's First Division side he joined Burnley on loan but at the end of that period he was immediately transferred to Swansea for £22,500 in September 1989.

He made his debut in a 6-1 defeat for the Swans against his home-town team Reading, but despite that he was almost a fixture in the Swans' defence in his six years at the Vetch.

In 1993-94, Harris was an ever-present in a mid-table Second Division campaign. In April 1994 he helped the Welsh club to victory in the Autoglass Trophy Final at Wembley when Huddersfield were finally overcome in a penalty shoot-out following a 1-1 draw after extra-time. He went on to score 18 goals in 288 games before moving to Gillingham.

In his first season with the Gills, he was a regular in the side that gained promotion to the Second Division, scoring the club's goal in the 1-1 draw against prospective champions Preston North End. He was released in the summer of 1997 and joined Cardiff City, but after just one month at Ninian Park in which the Bluebirds struggled, he was given a free transfer.

HARRIS, NEIL

Neil Harris was an aggressive centre-forward who played for Fulham as a 'guest' in their London Victory Cup Final of 1919 before joining Newcastle United from Partick Thistle in 1920. Harris possessed brilliant ball control and had a good eye for goal. He scored 103 goals in 194 first team games for the Magpies including one in their 2-0 FA Cup Final victory over Aston Villa in 1924. After leaving St James' Park, he played for Notts County, Oldham Athletic and Third Lanark before managing Distillery.

The Glasgow-born Harris arrived at the Vetch as Swansea's manager in the summer of 1934 but in his five seasons in charge, the club had a constant struggle to avoid relegation from the Second Division, having a best finish of 13th in 1935-36. At the beginning of June 1939, Harris announced his departure from the Vetch Field and took over at Swindon Town before the outbreak of the Second World War, but sadly he died whilst in office.

HARRISON, CHRIS

Chris Harrison became an apprentice with Plymouth Argyle at the age of 18 in October 1974 and made his Football League debut at right-back in the final match of the 1975-76 season. Over the next couple of seasons, he alternated between full-back and midfield before settling at full-back in 1979. Occasionally he also played in the centre of defence and over the next five seasons missed very few matches for the Pilgrims. After appearing in 371 League and Cup games for the Devon club, he lost his place and in September 1985 he was given a free transfer and joined Swansea.

In three seasons with the Vetch Field club, he scored 14 goals in 117 league games, first as a central defender and then at full-back linking up with another former Argyle player Colin Sullivan. While with the Swans, Harrison was also recognised as the team's penalty expert and ten of his goals for the Welsh club came from the spot. He left Swansea in the summer of 1988 and returned to the West Country to play for Saltash United.

HAT-TRICKS
A player by the name of Grier scored the club's first ever hat-trick in a match against Barry Town in the 1913-14 season.

After Ben Beynon had scored the club's first hat-trick in the Football League in a win over Norwich City on 16 September 1920, the club had to wait until 19 April 1922 when both W.Y. Brown and Jimmy Collins netted three goals apiece in an 8-0 win over Bristol Rovers. When the Swans beat Brentford 7-0 on 8 November 1924 Len Thompson scored four of the goals and Harry Deacon a hat-trick. The feat of two players scoring hat-tricks in the same match next occurred on 17 September 1927 when Lachlan McPherson and Jack Fowler each scored three goals in a 6-0 defeat of Wolverhampton Wanderers. It is Fowler who holds the club record for the most Football League hat-tricks with nine to his credit.

On Christmas Day 1929, Ronnie Williams was given his debut in the match against Notts County and responded by scoring a hat-trick. Another debutant to score a hat-trick was England international centre-forward Bob Latchford in the club's first ever Division One game against Leeds United on 29 August 1981 as the Yorkshire club were beaten 5-1. It took the Swansea striker just nine minutes 13 seconds - one of the quickest on record and the fastest by a Swansea player.

HAYES, MARTIN
Martin Hayes played for Waltham Forest and Essex Schoolboys before joining Arsenal as an apprentice in the summer of 1982. After working his way through the ranks he was named as substitute against Aston Villa in the final match of the 1982-83 season. However, he had to wait until 16 November 1985 before making his Arsenal league debut against Oxford United. In 1986-87 he was the club's leading scorer with 24 goals (12 of them being penalties - the most converted in one season by an Arsenal player).

He gained three England Under-21 caps and was outstanding in the League Cup Final of 1987 when the Gunners beat Liverpool. He began losing confidence and in May 1990 after scoring 34 goals in 138 League and Cup games he joined Celtic for £650,000.

The move was a disaster for both club and player as he appeared in just seven games with the Scottish club. Following a loan spell with Wimbledon he joined Swansea on a free transfer.

Hayes who made his debut against Fulham in January 1993, a match the Swans drew 2-2, spent two-and-a-half seasons at the Vetch Field, scoring eight goals in 61 league games before he left South Wales in the summer of 1995 to play non-league football for Dover Athletic.

HODGE, JOHN

Though he was born in Skelmersdale, winger John Hodge played non-league football for Falmouth Town before being given a chance at league level with Exeter City whom he joined in September 1991.

He went on to appear in 80 first team games for the Grecians, scoring 12 goals before joining Swansea in the summer of 1993 in a deal which took Russell Coughlin in the opposite direction.

He scored on his debut for the Swans in a 2-1 defeat at York City on the opening day of the 1993-94 season. He went on to appear in 26 league games that season but 11 of them were as a substitute. However, he did play at Wembley as Swansea beat Huddersfield Town in the final of the Autoglass Trophy.

On his day, Hodge is a difficult winger to play against, his exciting play bringing him 13 goals in 143 first team games before being given a free transfer in September 1996 and joining Walsall. A firm favourite at the Bescot Stadium, he has appeared in well over 100 games, his form in 1997-98 earning him selection for the award-winning PFA Second Division team.

HOLE, BARRIE

The son of pre-war Welsh international Billy Hole, one of the first league stars produced by Swansea, his two older brothers Colin and Alan both followed in their father's footsteps and played for their home-town club.

Barrie Hole did not follow the family tradition, preferring Cardiff City to his home-town club. He made his first team debut at 17 and quickly established himself as a creative wing-half and inside-forward. A Welsh Schoolboy international he went on to win five Under-23 caps before winning the first of 30 full caps against Northern Ireland in 1963. He had scored 16 goals in 211 league games for the Bluebirds when in the summer of 1966, he joined Blackburn Rovers for a fee of £40,000.

Although tall and slight in build, Hole was an extremely gifted ball-player. His intelligent positional play and constructive use of the ball made him one of the most exciting midfield players of his day. He had scored 15 goals in 88 League and Cup games for Rovers when in September 1968 he was transferred to Aston Villa for £60,000.

He left Villa Park midway through the 1969-70 season after a difficult time under Tommy Docherty's management. In fact, Hole turned his back on the game and went into his father's business.

During the summer of 1970, Roy Bentley the Swansea manager persuaded him to make a comeback, willingly paying Villa £20,000 to bring the Welsh international to the Vetch Field. He went on to play in 78 league games for the Swans before deciding to retire from the game in May 1972. Like his father, Barrie Hole then became a shopkeeper in Swansea.

HOLE, BILLY

A part-time professional, Billy Hole made his debut for the Swans against Brighton in October 1919, playing on the right-wing. He soon established himself as a first team regular and formed an outstanding right-wing pairing with Ivor Jones.

A great crowd favourite, he made a significant contribution to the history of Swansea Football Club, and on 9 April 1921 he became the first Swansea-born player to be selected for his country while playing for his home-town club. In fact, he scored on his international debut at the Vetch as Wales beat Ireland 2-1.

With the exception of 1923-24 when an early season injury kept him out of action for virtually the whole of the campaign, he was a first team regular for 12 seasons. He returned midway through the following season to help the Swans win the Third Division (South) Championship.

Hole, who left the Vetch in the summer of 1931, provided many of the crosses from which Jack Fowler scored a number of his goals, though he did his fair share of scoring from the wing, with 40 goals in 341 league games. Billy Hole's three sons, Colin, Alan and Barrie all wore the white shirt of Swansea.

HOLLINS, JOHN

John Hollins comes from a footballing family with three of his brothers, his father and grandfather having played league football.

He joined Chelsea as a 15-year-old in the summer of 1961 and turned professional two years later when almost immediately he won a regular place in the Stamford Bridge side. An outstanding, attacking wing-half, he served Chelsea with great distinction for 12 seasons, taking part in all the club's successes in that period.

He won just one cap for England against Spain in May 1967 shortly after playing in a losing FA Cup Final against Spurs. He won an FA Cup winners' medal in 1970 against Leeds United and the following year Chelsea won the European Cup Winners' Cup Final against Real Madrid in Athens, though he missed the replay.

After Chelsea were relegated, Hollins left and joined Queen's Park

John Hollins

Rangers for £80,000 and in 1975-76, his first season with the Loftus Road club, he helped them to the runners-up spot in the First Division. He served them well for another four seasons before surprisingly joining Arsenal where he went on to appear in 172 League and Cup games before being given a free transfer at the age of 36.

He returned to Stamford Bridge as player-coach and in his first season helped them win promotion to the First Division. He retired at the end of the 1983-84 season when he was appointed team coach, later becoming manager in June 1985.

Hollins who was awarded the MBE for his services to football in 1981, appeared in 465 league games for Chelsea, scoring 48 goals. As a manager, he was not popular with the Chelsea fans due to his teams being efficient but dull! However, he was treated badly by Chelsea Chairman Ken Bates who brought in Bobby Campbell as coach without his knowledge, and in March 1988, he resigned.

After a spell as a financial adviser, he returned to the game as reserve team coach at Queen's Park Rangers in February 1995 before being appointed Swansea manager in July 1998. In his first season at the Vetch he led the Swans to the fourth round of the FA Cup after they had beaten Premier League opposition in West Ham United in round three, and to the Third Division play-offs.

HOME MATCHES

Swansea's best home wins are the 12-0 rout of Sliema Wanderers from Malta in a first round first leg European Cup Winners' Cup tie on 15 September 1982 and the 8-0 defeat of Hartlepool United in a Fourth Division match played on 1 April 1978.

The club's worst home defeat is 6-1, a scoreline inflicted upon the club by four visitors to the Vetch Field - Bradford Park Avenue on 14 September 1946, Workington on 14 September 1965, Reading on 23 September 1989 and Wigan Athletic on 6 April 1991.

HOME SEASONS

The club's longest league run of home wins is 17 in season 1948-49 when they won the Third Division (South) Championship and ended the campaign undefeated at the Vetch, winning 20 and drawing one of their games.

Swansea's longest run of matches without a home win is nine in 1938, whilst the club's longest league run of undefeated home matches is 28 set between 1925 and 1927.

HOUGH, DAVID

Crewe-born defender David Hough, who had moved to South Wales with his parents as a child, played in the Swans' Youth Championship side of 1982-83 before making his full first team debut at Portsmouth in the final game of the following season, a match the Swans lost 5-0.

A former Welsh Youth international, he made his mark in the Vetch club's side in the right-back position but also showed his worth in the centre of defence.

Strong in the tackle, he enjoyed nothing more than pushing forward on the overlap and crossing the ball from the by-line.

By the time he played the last of his 227 league games in which he scored nine goals, at Fulham in September 1991, he was the longest-serving player on the Vetch Field staff.

HUGHES, BRIAN

Tough-tackling wing-half Brian Hughes worked his way up through the club's junior teams before making his first team debut for the Swans during the 1958-59 season. Hughes who won two caps for Wales at Under-23 level, was a member of the Swansea side that created a little bit of history in January 1959 when they played Fulham at Craven Cottage. Eight of the side were full internationals while three, of which Hughes was one, had won Under-23 or Youth caps.

Over the years, Hughes had a number of outstanding games, but perhaps none more so than when the Swans beat Liverpool 2-1 at Anfield in the FA Cup sixth round tie of 1963-64. Hughes was a member of the Swansea side for ten seasons but in January 1969 after he had scored six goals in 231 league games he left the club to join Atlanta Chiefs in the United States.

HUMPHRIES, WILLIE

At school, Willie Humphries was a rugby scrum-half but also shone as a soccer player and joined Glentoran as an amateur while working as a clerical officer with the Belfast Transport department. His career took off when he joined Ards, and Leeds United beat Blackpool to his signature in September 1958. He failed to settle at Elland Road and returned to Ards in November 1959.

It was Coventry City manager Jimmy Hill who persuaded Humphries to have another attempt playing in the Football League. The Irishman had a couple of outstanding seasons on the right-wing, both scoring and making goals on a regular basis. A Northern Ireland international, winning four caps, he helped the Sky Blues to win promotion to the Second Division. But in March 1965 after scoring 24 goals in 126 games, he joined Swansea for a fee of £14,000.

Although he was unable to keep the Welsh club in the Second Division, he had three good seasons at the Vetch Field, scoring 22 goals in 143 league games before returning to Ireland for his third and longest spell with Ards. During those years he was 'Footballer of the Year' for the Irish League and his side won the Cup. Humphries later managed Bangor from 1983 to 1985 before buying a newsagents business which he ran until he retired in 1991.

HUTCHISON, TOMMY

One of the most naturally gifted players of the post-war era, Scottish international Tommy Hutchison began his career with Alloa before Blackpool brought him into League football in 1968.

In 1969-70 he helped the Seasiders win promotion to the First Division, laying on countless chances for his team-mates. However, success was short-lived and Blackpool were relegated after just one season in the top flight. Hutchison continued to impress with his close control, pin-point crosses and his ability to beat a player with skill and pace, and it came as no surprise when he joined Coventry City in October 1972.

In 1973 he won the first of 17 full Scottish caps, all whilst with the Highfield Road club. In an eight year stay with the Sky Blues, Hutchison scored 24 goals in 314 league games before leaving to join Manchester City.

One of John Bond's most influential signings, he helped the Maine Road club to the semi-final of the League Cup and the epic FA Cup Final against Tottenham Hotspur in 1981. During that match he headed City into a first-half lead only to have the misfortune to score a late equaliser for Spurs when he deflected Glenn Hoddle's shot past Joe Corrigan.

He left Maine Road in the summer of 1982 to spend a season in Hong Kong before signing for Burnley, where he appeared in 92 league games. Never fully accepted by the Turf Moor crowd, he joined Swansea in July 1985.

He made his debut for the Swans against Wigan Athletic at the Vetch on the opening day of the 1985-86 season, later becoming player-coach but also played his part in the Vetch Field club's promotion to the Third Division in 1987-88. During that season he spent a brief spell on loan at Blackpool, almost 20 years after he had first played for the Seasiders.

In 1988-89 he was virtually an ever-present and competed in the European Cup Winners' Cup in 1989-90 at the age of 42, the oldest player ever to play in a European tie. In March 1991 he played the last of his 178 league games for the Swans at the age of 43 years and 171 days and at the end of the season, received a PFA Merit Award for his services to football after 860 league appearances for his five clubs.

The popular Scot then became Football in the Community Officer at Merthyr Tydfil, passing on his vast knowledge of the game at coaching sessions throughout South Wales.

Tommy Hutchison

I

INTERNATIONAL MATCHES
Vetch Field has hosted 18 full international football matches with the first between Wales and Ireland being played on 9 April 1921 when the home side won 2-1. Wales played their first international in South Wales on 24 February 1894 when Ireland were again their opponents, only on that occasion the venue was St Helen's, half a mile away from the Vetch.

INTERNATIONAL PLAYERS
Swansea City's most capped player (ie: caps gained while players were registered with the club) is Ivor Allchurch with 42 caps. The following is a complete list of players who have gained full international honours whilst with the Swans:

Wales
Ivor Allchurch (42)

> 1951 v England, N.Ireland, Portugal, Switzerland
> 1952 v England, Scotland, Rest of UK, N.Ireland
> 1953 v Scotland, England, N.Ireland, France, Yugoslavia
> 1954 v Scotland, England, N.Ireland, Austria
> 1955 v Scotland, England, N.Ireland, Yugoslavia
> 1956 v England, Scotland, N.Ireland, Austria
> 1957 v England, Scotland
> 1958 v N.Ireland, Israel(2), Hungary(2), Mexico, Sweden, Brazil

1966 v USSR, England, Scotland, Denmark, Brazil(2), Chile

Len Allchurch (7)
    1955 v N.Ireland
    1956 v Austria
    1958 v Scotland, N.Ireland, East Germany, Israel
    1959 v Scotland

Jason Bowen (1)
    1994 v Estonia

Jeremy Charles (12)
    1981 v Czechoslovakia, Turkey, Scotland, USSR
    1982 v Iceland
    1983 v Norway, Yugoslavia, Bulgaria, Scotland, N.Ireland, Brazil
    1984 v Bulgaria

Mel Charles (21)
    1955 v N.Ireland
    1956 v England, Scotland, Austria
    1957 v England, Czechoslovakia (2), N.Ireland, East Germany
    1958 v England, Scotland, East Germany, Israel(2), Hungary(2),
           Mexico, Sweden, Brazil
    1959 v England, Scotland

John Cornforth (2)
    1995 v Bulgaria, Germany

Alan Curtis (23)
    1976 v England(2), Yugoslavia(2), Scotland, N.Ireland
    1977 v West Germany, Scotland, N.Ireland
    1978 v West Germany, England, Scotland
    1979 v West Germany, Scotland
    1982 v Czechoslovakia, Iceland, USSR, Spain, England, Scotland,
           N.Ireland
    1983 v Norway, Romania

Alan Davies (3)
    1988 v Malta, Italy

1989 v Holland

Dai Davies (8)
    1982 v Czechoslovakia, Iceland, USSR, Spain, England, Scotland, France
    1983 v Yugoslavia

Willie Davies (3)
    1924 v England, Scotland, N.Ireland

Chris Edwards (1)
    1996 v Switzerland

Brian Evans (6)
    1972 v Finland, Czechoslovakia
    1973 v England(2), Poland, Scotland

Roy Evans (1)
    1964 v N.Ireland

Trevor Ford (1)
    1947 v Scotland

Jack Fowler (6)
    1925 v England
    1926 v England, N.Ireland
    1927 v Scotland
    1928 v Scotland
    1929 v England

David Giles (9)
    1980 v England, Scotland, N.Ireland, Iceland
    1981 v Turkey(2), Czechoslovakia, England, USSR

Harry Griffiths (1)
    1953 v N.Ireland

Harry Hanford (3)
    1934 v N.Ireland

> 1935 v Scotland
> 1936 v England

Barrie Hole (1)
> 1971 v Romania

Billy Hole (9)
> 1921 v N.Ireland
> 1922 v England
> 1923 v England, N.Ireland
> 1928 v England, Scotland, N.Ireland
> 1929 v England, Scotland

Leighton James (16)
> 1980 v England, Scotland, N.Ireland, Iceland
> 1981 v Turkey(2), Eire, Scotland, England
> 1982 v Czechoslovakia, Iceland, England, USSR, Scotland,
>   N.Ireland, France

Robbie James (19)
> 1979 v Malta(2), West Germany, Scotland, England, N.Ireland
> 1980 v West Germany
> 1982 v Czechoslovakia, Iceland, Spain, England, Scotland,
>   N.Ireland, France
> 1983 v Norway, Yugoslavia, England, Bulgaria
> 1988 v Yugoslavia

Steve Jenkins (1)
> 1996 v Germany

Roy John (2)
> 1939 v England, Scotland

Michael Johnson (1)
> 1964 v N.Ireland

Barrie Jones (7)
> 1963 v Scotland, England N.Ireland, Hungary(2)
> 1964 v Scotland, N.Ireland

Cliff Jones (16)
> 1954 v Austria
> 1956 v England, N.Ireland, Scotland, Austria
> 1957 v England, Scotland, N.Ireland, Czechoslovakia(2),
>   East Germany
> 1958 v East Germany, England, Scotland, Israel(2)

Ivor Jones (6)
> 1920 v Scotland, N.Ireland
> 1921 v England, N.Ireland
> 1922 v Scotland, N.Ireland

Ernie Jones (2)
> 1947 v England, Scotland

John King (1)
> 1955 v England

Alan Knill (1)
> 1989 v Holland

Sid Lawrence (8)
> 1932 v N.Ireland
> 1933 v France
> 1934 v Scotland, England, N.Ireland
> 1935 v England, Scotland
> 1936 v Scotland

Dai Lewis (2)
> 1933 v England, Scotland

Dudley Lewis (1)
> 1983 v Brazil

Wilf Lewis (5)
> 1927 v England, N.Ireland
> 1928 v England, N.Ireland
> 1929 v Scotland

Billy Lucas (7)
    1949 v Scotland, N.Ireland, Portugal, Belgium, Switzerland
    1950 v England
    1951 v England

John Mahoney (7)
    1980 v Eire, West Germany, Turkey
    1982 v Iceland, USSR
    1983 v Yugoslavia, England

Chris Marustik (6)
    1980 v Spain, England, Scotland, N.Ireland, France
    1983 v Norway

Terry Medwin (3)
    1953 v N.Ireland, France, Yugoslavia

Andy Melville (4)
    1990 v West Germany, Eire, Sweden, Costa Rica

Tony Millington (8)
    1970 v England, Scotland, N.Ireland
    1971 v Czechoslovakia, Finland
    1972 v Finland, Czechoslovakia, Romania

John Morgan (2)
    1879 v Scotland
    1883 v England

Ernie Morley (1)
    1925 v England

Dai Nicholas (2)
    1927 v England, N.Ireland

Mel Nurse (9)
    1960 v England, N.Ireland
    1961 v Scotland, England, Holland, N.Ireland, Eire, Spain(2)

Des Palmer (3)
> 1957 v Czechoslovakia
> 1958 v England, East Germany

Jack Parry (1)
> 1951 v Scotland

Colin Pascoe (2)
> 1984 v Norway, Israel

Roy Paul (9)
> 1949 v England, Scotland, N.Ireland, Portugal, Switzerland
> 1950 v England, Scotland, N.Ireland, Belgium

Leighton Phillips (18)
> 1979 v Turkey, West Germany, Scotland, England, N.Ireland,
> Malta
> 1980 v Eire, West Germany, Turkey, Scotland, N.Ireland, Iceland
> 1981 v Turkey(2), Czechoslovakia, Scotland, England, USSR

Frankie Scrine (2)
> 1950 v England, N.Ireland

Nigel Stevenson (4)
> 1982 v England, Scotland, N.Ireland
> 1983 v Norway

Dai Thomas (2)
> 1957 v Czechoslovakia
> 1958 v East Germany

John Toshack (6)
> 1979 v West Germany, Scotland, England, N.Ireland, Malta
> 1980 v West Germany

Ian Walsh (4)
> 1982 v Spain, Scotland, N.Ireland, France

Jack Warner (1)
    1937 v England

Ben Williams (4)
    1928 v N.Ireland, England
    1930 v England, Scotland

Graham Williams (5)
    1961 v N.Ireland, Hungary, Spain(2)
    1962 v England

Herbie Williams (3)
    1965 v Greece(2)
    1972 v Romania

Northern Ireland
Hugh Blair (1)
    1934 v Scotland

Ronnie Briggs (1)
    1965 v Holland

Jim Feeney (1)
    1950 v England

Willie Humphries (2)
    1965 v Wales, Albania

Rory Keane (1)
    1949 v Scotland

Jimmy McLaughlin (7)
    1964 v Wales, Uruguay
    1965 v England, Wales, Switzerland(2)
    1966 v Wales

Jackie O'Driscoll (3)
    1949 v England, Scotland, Wales

Republic of Ireland
Noel Dwyer (10)
      1961 v Wales, Norway, Scotland (2)
      1962 v Czechoslovakia (2)
      1964 v Poland, Norway, England
      1965 v Poland

Rory Keane (4)
      1949 v Switzerland, Portugal, Sweden, Spain

Jackie O'Driscoll (3)
      1949 v Switzerland, Belgium, Sweden

J

JAMES, LEIGHTON

One of the game's most naturally gifted players, Leighton James represented Swansea Boys and then was chosen for the Welsh Schoolboy International team before signing for Burnley as an apprentice in October 1968. He soon established himself in the Clarets' first team, his sparkling performances on the wing inevitably alerting the international selectors.

He won the first of 54 Welsh caps in October 1971 against Czechoslovakia in Prague, the youngest Burnley international and one of the youngest players ever to be capped for Wales. He won a Second Division Championship medal in 1972-73 but after two good seasons in the top flight, Leighton James was off on his travels.

Dave Mackay paid a club record £310,000 to take him to Derby County and he was top scorer at the Baseball Ground in 1976-77 before moving to Queen's Park Rangers. After less than a year at Loftus Road he returned to Turf Moor for £165,000, a record for Burnley that stood until 1994. Following Burnley's relegation to Division Three, James moved on again, this time to ambitious Swansea for £130,000.

He was an instant success in his homeland and was top scorer as the Swans finished third to gain promotion to the top flight for the first time in the club's history. Included in his total were two hat-tricks, the first against his former club Derby County on 11 October 1980 and the second in a 3-0 win over Bolton Wanderers on 28 February 1981. In this latter match, he converted two penalties and then hit home a 25-yard screamer.

James also played a key role in Swansea's victory in the Welsh Cup with its passport to Europe. James had scored 27 goals in 98 league games when he moved to Sunderland on a free transfer in January 1983.

He returned to play in the north-west with Bury in the summer of 1984 and was ever-present as the Shakers gained promotion to Division Three. After just over a year at Gigg Lane he joined Newport County as player-coach before returning to Burnley for a third spell in July 1986. He was top scorer with 10 goals and was instrumental in the club's great escape against Orient in May 1987.

After coaching at Bradford City, he entered non-league management first with Gainsborough Trinity and then Morecambe. James who scored 123 goals in 656 league games for his seven clubs is now a regular on Lancashire radio sports programmes.

Leighton James

JAMES, ROBBIE

It was Swansea manager Harry Gregg who signed Robbie James on amateur forms and after the talented youngster had impressed in Welsh League and Football Combination games, he was given his first team debut in the final match of the 1972-73 season against Charlton Athletic. James, who was just 16 years old, starred in a 2-1 win for the Swans.

The driving midfielder was instrumental in the club's rise from the Fourth Division to the First Division and in 1979 his form led to him winning the first of 47 full caps for Wales when he played against Malta.

Within the space of 12 months during the club's successive promotions, James netted three hat-tricks against Hartlepool United in the Football League (Home 8-0 on 25 April 1978), Newport County in the League Cup (Home 5-0 on 15 August 1978) and Kidderminster Harriers in the Welsh Cup (Home 6-1 on 29 January 1979).

Robbie James

He had scored 99 goals in 394 league games for Swansea when in July 1983 after the club had lost their place in the top flight, he joined Stoke City for £160,000. Never quite able to produce the goods, he left the Potters in October 1984, signing for Queen's Park Rangers for a fee of £100,000. At Loftus Road he was used successfully as a full-back before moving to Leicester City where he provided valuable experience to the Filbert Street club's young defence. In January 1988 with his pace waning, he was released and returned to the Vetch Field for a second spell.

In 1987-88 he captained the Swans to promotion to the Third Division but after taking his total of league goals to 115 in 484 appearances, he left the Vetch a second time to join Bradford City in the summer of 1990 as part of a deal involving Alan Davies in settlement of the Welsh club's outstanding court action against manager Terry Yorath. After leaving Valley Parade, James played non-league football but died tragically while playing for Llanelli in a Welsh League match, aged just 40.

JENKINS, STEVE

Steve Jenkins is a solid defender who turned professional in the summer of 1990 after a two year apprenticeship. He made his debut as a substitute against Cambridge United in the last game of the 1990-91 season. In just over five seasons at the Vetch, the dependable Jenkins played in 215 first team games with his only goal for the club coming in a 1-1 home draw against Hartlepool United in January 1991. Having won Welsh Youth and Under-21 honours, he made his first full appearance for his country against West Germany at Cardiff, but soon after was on his way to Huddersfield Town for a fee of £275,000 - a low tribunal judgement.

On his debut for the Yorkshire club, he was played on the right-wing and scored in a 3-2 home win over Norwich City. He then settled into the Terriers side at right-back and over the next couple of seasons took his total of Welsh caps to 10 as well as being rewarded with the captaincy of the Huddersfield side.

JOHNSON, MIKE

A former Swansea Schoolboy player, he worked his way up through the club's ranks to make his first team debut during the 1959-60 season, though his early years at the Vetch Field were spent as an understudy to Mel Nurse. However, whenever he did play for Swansea, centre-half Johnson always gave a committed and polished performance and in view of this, the club let Nurse join Middlesbrough in September 1962.

91

Johnson's performances won him two Welsh Under-23 caps and in April 1964 he won full international honours when he played against Northern Ireland at Ninian Park. Johnson had also by this time, not only become the club's regular centre-half but also club captain and in his first game as skipper led the Swans to a 4-1 win over Barrow. Johnson only scored one goal during his 168 league appearances but his defensive displays certainly reduced the opportunities for the opposition forwards to score.

JONES, BARRIE
Swansea-born Barrie Jones began his career with his home-town team as a winger in the traditional mould. In five years at the Vetch Field he was capped eight times at Welsh Under-23 level and won the first of 15 full caps when he played against Scotland at Ninian Park in October 1962.

Jones who possessed pace and a powerful shot, had scored 23 goals in 166 games when he was transferred to Plymouth Argyle for £45,000 in September 1964. It was then the Devon club's highest ever payment for a player. It was Jones' exceptional ball-control which Argyle manager Malcolm Allison was seeking to incorporate into his team plans, but in March 1967, Jones, who had scored nine goals in 99 league outings, returned to South Wales and to Cardiff City for a fee of £25,000.

An ever-present in seasons 1967-68 and 1968-69, Jones was moved into midfield with great success, winning seven more Welsh caps, compared to one cap whilst with Plymouth. On 4 October 1969 Jones broke his leg in the last minute of the Bluebirds game at Blackpool and though he attempted a number of comebacks, he never regained full fitness, and though he played for a number of seasons at non-league level, his Football League days were over.

JONES, BRYN
One of the members of the famous Jones footballing family, being the son of Ivor and the brother of Cliff, Bryn Jones made his first team debut for the Swans during the 1952-53 season.

Though the full-back never really established himself in his six seasons at the Vetch he gave loyal service and had appeared in 121 league games when in the summer of 1958 he left to join Newport County. In two seasons at Somerton Park in which he was occasionally played at wing-half, he scored 11 goals in 71 games before signing for Bournemouth.

He was a great favourite with the Dean Court crowd, appearing in 118 league games and helping the Cherries to a best position of third in Division Three in 1961-62 before leaving to join Northampton Town. His stay at the County Ground lasted just one month before he was on the move again, this time to Watford where he ended his league career having played in 408 games for his five clubs.

JONES, CLIFF

Cliff Jones was the fourth member of his family to make his name in professional football following his father Ivor who played for Swansea Town, West Bromwich Albion and Wales, his uncle Bryn who played for Wolverhampton Wanderers, Norwich City, Arsenal and Wales and his brother Bryn, who played for Swansea Town, Newport County, Bournemouth, Northampton Town and Watford.

He first came to prominence when Swansea defeated Manchester to win the Schools Shield. Having signed for Swansea Town in 1952 he made his first team debut in October of that year and in six and a half

Cliff Jones

93

seasons at the Vetch Field, he scored 47 goals in 168 league games. He won his first full cap for Wales against Austria in May 1954 when just turned 19 and became one of the most exciting players in the game. By the time of his transfer to Tottenham Hotspur in February 1958 he had won 16 caps, yet it was only after moving to White Hart Lane that he began to train on a full-time basis!

A member of the Welsh side that did so well in the 1958 World Cup in Sweden, he broke his leg in a pre-season training collision with Peter Baker but survived the setback to become an indispensable member of the Spurs side, capable of playing on either wing or at inside-forward.

One of the most popular figures in Tottenham's history, he thrilled the supporters with his courage, pace and goalscoring feats. A key member of the famous team that won the 'double' in 1960-61, the FA Cup in 1961-62 and the European Cup Winners' Cup in 1962-63, he picked up another FA Cup winners' medal in the 1967 final as the first non-playing substitute. He added another 41 caps to the 16 he won with Swansea and represented the Football League on three occasions. In October 1968 his great service to Spurs was recognised with a £5,000 cut-price transfer to Fulham, where he won his final two caps.

JOHN, DILWYN

Goalkeeper Dilwyn John began his league career with Cardiff City and was just 17 years 109 days old when he made his debut for the Bluebirds in a 3-2 win at Chelsea on 20 September 1961. Over the next six seasons, John played in 99 first team games and won a Welsh Under-23 cap but his slender physique meant that he never developed into one of Welsh football's greatest goalkeepers.

In March 1967 he left Ninian Park and joined Swansea and in almost four seasons at Vetch Field, he made 80 league appearances. Initially he helped stem the flow of goals that the Swansea defence had been leaking but despite some heroic performances, he couldn't prevent the club's relegation to Division Four. However, he helped the club win promotion in 1969-70 before leaving to play non-league football for both Hereford United and Merthyr Tydfil.

JONES, ERNIE

Ernie 'Alphabet' Jones began his career as an amateur with Swansea but turned professional with Bolton Wanderers. After failing to win a place in the Lancashire club's league team, he returned to Swansea during the

Second World War and quickly built a big reputation as a fast and clever attacking winger. He won the first of four Welsh caps against Scotland in October 1946 and collected a second before leaving the Vetch to join Tottenham Hotspur for £7,000 in June 1947.

In two years at White Hart Lane, Jones scored 16 goals in 65 games and won two more caps before losing his place to Les Medley. In May 1949 he moved to Southampton as part of the deal that took Alf Ramsey to Spurs. He served the Saints for two years before a transfer to Bristol City, where he ended his league career.

After hanging up his boots, he managed Rhyl Town where he even helped to design and erect the floodlights before later spending two years coaching the juniors at Southampton.

JONES, IVOR

Ivor Jones was the first of a family connection with his two sons, Cliff and Bryn following later. Signed as a teenager from Caerphilly for whom he had impressed against the Swans' Reserves, he was to captivate the Vetch Field crowds with his brilliance.

He won the first of 10 full caps for Wales when he played against Ireland in 1920, thus becoming the first Swansea player to represent his country whilst with the club, despite having only played in 14 Southern League games. One of the club's most skilful players of that time, he had scored 14 goals in 66 league games, when he was surprisingly sold to West Bromwich Albion for a club record fee of £2,500 - a decision that the Swansea supporters did not take kindly to.

JUBILEE FUND

The League Benevolent Fund was launched in 1938, fifty years after the start of the Football League, to benefit players who had fallen on hard times. It was decided that the best way to raise funds was for sides to play local 'derby' games with no account being taken of league status. Swansea played Cardiff City at the Vetch Field before the start of the 1938-39 season and shared six goals. The return game played at Ninian Park just before the ill-fated 1939-40 season also ended all-square at 1-1.

K

KEANE, RORY

Limerick-born full-back Rory Keane joined Swansea from his home-town club in the summer of 1947. The strong-tackling Irishman soon established himself in the Swansea side where his robust performances soon won him international recognition. He made his debut for the Republic of Ireland against Switzerland in 1949 and over the season made a further three appearances. Also in that 1949-50 season he became one of the few players to have represented both the Republic and Northern Ireland when he played for the latter against Scotland at Hampden Park.

Towards the end of that season, Keane fractured a leg and though he returned to first team action the following term, he was never the same player.

He stayed at the Vetch for nine seasons, appearing in 164 league games. Though he failed to score for the club, he did execute a number of goal-line clearances to prevent certain goals, and in the FA Cup fourth round tie against Arsenal at Highbury in 1949-50, he punched the ball over the bar from a Lewis header when it was almost over the line! Unfortunately, the Gunners scored from the resultant penalty and went on to win 2-1.

KENNEDY, RAY

After being rejected by Port Vale, Ray Kennedy joined Arsenal and shot to fame when he scored one of the Gunners' goals in the second leg of the European Fairs Final. The following season he became a first team regular and was Arsenal's leading scorer with 26 goals in 63 games as well as winning England Under-23 honours. With John Radford he formed one of the league's deadliest goalscoring partnerships and in a further three seasons at Highbury went on to score 71 goals in 212 League and Cup games before in July 1974 he was transferred to Liverpool for £200,000.

He was a disappointment in his early days at Anfield but blossomed after Bob Paisley converted him into a midfielder.

He went on to win countless honours at Anfield plus 17 England caps, adding European medals to the domestic ones he had already won at Arsenal.

In January 1982 in the face of severe competition from Stoke and Sunderland, Kennedy joined Swansea for a fee of £160,000 and made his debut against Manchester United in front of the Vetch Field's highest crowd of the season, 23,900. His presence in midfield was instrumental in the Swans winning 2-0, as he set up goals for Alan Curtis and Leighton James. The Swans were unbeaten in Kennedy's first nine games for the club and though he only appeared in 42 league games, scoring two goals, before returning to his native north-east to play for Hartlepool United, he was a popular figure at the Vetch.

It was later discovered that he had Parkinson's Disease and a special match was staged between Arsenal and Liverpool to finance his medical treatment.

KILEY, TOM

A member of the Swansea Schoolboys side before the Second World War, he went on to make three appearances for the Welsh international schoolboys team before joining the RAF. At the end of the hostilities, he was included in the Welsh League side and on leaving the RAF in 1947, joined Swansea.

His first few years at the Vetch Field were spent in Welsh League and Combination football and eventually after a series of good performances, he made his first team debut in a goalless draw at Queen's Park Rangers on Good Friday 1950.

A tall and commanding centre-half, Kiley suffered a number of injuries whilst at the Vetch and in February 1953 fractured his leg. However, he regained full fitness and in 1954-55 was selected as a reserve for the full Welsh side.

In November 1956, Kiley suffered a serious knee injury in training and landed in hospital where he underwent an operation. He didn't return to first team action until March 1957 but unfortunately the popular defender only played in a handful of games before he was forced to retire.

There is no doubt that the injury to Kiley, who played in 130 league games, cost the club promotion to the First Division, as he was the lynch-pin of the Swansea defence.

KING, JOHN

John King holds the club appearance record for a goalkeeper with 368 league appearances under his belt between 1950 and 1964.

He made his debut as a 17-year-old amateur in a 5-0 defeat at Birmingham City on 16 December 1950. After his National Service, King proved himself to be one of the best 'keepers outside the top flight and in 1955 won the only full cap of his career when he played in a 2-1 win over England at Ninian Park.

Up until the arrival of Noel Dwyer in 1960, King was a virtual ever-present in the Swansea side, but following the Irishman's performances when he deputised for King, he had to be content to share the goalkeeping duties. In February 1961, King was awarded a £1,000 benefit following a superb performance against Preston North End in the fourth round of that seasons FA Cup.

The popular 'keeper later emigrated to Australia where he died aged just 49 in 1982.

KNILL, ALAN

A former apprentice with Southampton, Alan Knill failed to make the grade at The Dell and in the summer of 1984, joined Halifax Town.

He made his league debut for the Shaymen against Blackpool on 25 August 1984 and ended the season playing in 44 games. Knill was a virtual ever-present in his three seasons with the Yorkshire club but in August 1987 after appearing in 136 games for Halifax he joined Swansea for a tribunal fixed fee of £15,000.

He made his debut in a 2-0 win at Stockport County on the opening day of the 1987-88 season and formed an effective central defensive partnership, first with Andy Melville and then Dudley Lewis. In his first season with the club, the Swans gained promotion via the play-offs to the Third Division, whilst in 1988-89 they came close to winning another play-off place. Also during that season, Knill's performances led to him winning an international cap for Wales when he was chosen to play against Holland in Amsterdam in a World Cup qualifying game.

At the end of the 1988-89 season, Knill who had appeared in 105 first team games for the Vetch Field club decided to take up the offer of a contract from Bury, claiming that Swansea lacked ambition. Once again his fee was settled by a tribunal, this time £95,000, Bury's record outgoing transfer fee.

In four seasons at Gigg Lane, he played in two consecutive play-off finals, suffered relegation to the league's basement and then appeared in another play-off match against York City. Knill who had played in 174 games for Bury had a short loan spell with Cardiff City before joining Scunthorpe United. He made 154 appearances for the Irons before joining Rotherham United in the summer of 1997.

L

LALLY, PAT

Paddington-born wing-half Pat Lally began his footballing career with Millwall but in the summer of 1971, after making just one league appearance for the Lions, he joined York City. After two seasons at Bootham Crescent in which he was a virtual ever-present, Lally signed for Swansea for a fee of £8,000.

He made his debut for the Vetch Field club in a 2-0 home win over Chester on the opening day of the 1973-74 season and over the next five seasons, missed very few games.

The midfielder made a great contribution to the Welsh side and in 1977-78 helped them win promotion to the Third Division after finishing third in Division Four with 56 points.

At the end of that season, Lally, who had scored 10 goals in 160 league games was surprisingly allowed to leave the Vetch and join Doncaster Rovers for £10,000.

During his time at Bellev Vue, Lally took his total of appearances to 357 before injury forced his retirement.

LARGEST CROWD

It was on 17 February 1968 that the Vetch Field housed its largest crowd. The occasion was the fourth round FA Cup match against Arsenal. A staggering crowd of 32,796 saw the Gunners win 1-0.

LATCHFORD, BOB

A big, bustling centre-forward, Bob Latchford made his name with his home-town club Birmingham City, for whom he scored 68 goals in 160 league games. He signed for Everton in February 1974 for a fee of £350,000 and made his debut in a 4-3 defeat at West Ham United. In his first four full seasons with the Goodison club, Latchford was the top league goalscorer, reaching his peak in 1977-78 when he became the first Division One player for six years to reach the 30-goal mark. His total included four in a 5-1 win at Queen's Park Rangers. Latchford reached the final game of the season at home to Chelsea needing two goals to claim a national newspaper prize of £10,000. Everton won 6-0 and Latchford net-ted the goals necessary to win the money and carve a place for himself in Merseyside football folklore.

Bob Latchford

Whilst at Goodison, Latchford won 12 full international caps for England. In the summer of 1981 after scoring 138 goals in 289 League and Cup games, he left to join Swansea for £125,000.

He made a remarkable debut in the club's first-ever game in the top flight, scoring a second-half hat-trick inside the space of ten minutes as Leeds United were beaten 5-1 in front of a Vetch Field crowd of 23,489. In 1982-83 he scored 23 goals including hat-tricks against Norwich City (Home 4-0) and Bristol Rovers (Home 3-0) in what was a second round second leg League Cup tie. He had scored 35 goals in 87 games for the Swans when he was given a free transfer and joined Dutch club NAC Breda. Within five months he had returned to England and signed for Coventry City. Twelve months later he left to play for Lincoln City, before ending his career with Newport County.

LAWRENCE, SID

Promising young full-back Sid Lawrence worked his way up through the ranks to make his first team debut for the Swans midway through the 1930-31 season. He soon established himself in the Vetch Field club's defence and by 1932-33 his impressive form not only made him the subject of transfer rumours from top flight clubs but also won him his first cap for Wales when he played against Northern Ireland. He continued to impress and was without doubt, one of the most effective performers in the club's defence. Lawrence went on to win eight full caps for his country, making his last appearance against Scotland in 1936.

After scoring 11 goals, most of them long-range shots in 312 league appearances for the Swans, he was made available for transfer in the spring of 1939. Lawrence followed his former manager at the Vetch Field, Neil Harris to Swindon Town, where he ended his career.

LEADING GOALSCORERS

Swansea have provided the Football League's divisional leading goalscorer on three occasions. They are:

1924-25	Jack Fowler	Division Three(South)	28 goals
1931-32	Cyril Pearce	Division Two	35 goals
1977-78*	Alan Curtis	Division Four	32 goals

* Tied with Brentford's Steve Phillips

LEAGUE GOALS - CAREER HIGHEST
Ivor Allchurch holds the Vetch Field record for the most league goals with a career total of 166 goals between 1949-1958 and 1965-1968.

LEAGUE GOALS - LEAST CONCEDED
During the 1948-49 season, the Swans conceded just 34 goals in 42 games when they won the Third Division (South) Championship.

LEAGUE GOALS - MOST INDIVIDUAL
Cyril Pearce holds the Swansea record for the most league goals in a season with 35 scored in 1931-32 when the Vetch Field club finished 15th in the Second Division.

LEAGUE GOALS - MOST SCORED
Swansea's highest goal tally in the Football League was during the 1976-77 Fourth Division campaign when they scored 92 goals and finished fifth.

LEAGUE VICTORY - HIGHEST
Swansea's best league victory is the 8-0 win over Hartlepool United in a Fourth Division game at Vetch Field on 1 April 1978. Both Robbie James and Alan Curtis hit hat-tricks whilst the Swans' other goals were scored by John Toshack and Les Chappell.

LEGG, ANDY
Andy Legg played for non-league Briton Ferry before moving to the Vetch Field in August 1988. A fast and tricky winger who enjoys taking on defenders, he was an important member of the Swansea side for five seasons, scoring 38 goals in 207 League and Cup games before leaving the Welsh club to join Notts County for a fee of £275,000.

After appearing in 126 first team games in two and a half seasons at Meadow Lane, he was transferred to Birmingham City along with Paul Devlin and soon settled down on the left-hand side of the St Andrews club's midfield. A long-throw specialist, his world record throw of 44.54 metres was beaten in 1996-97 by Tranmere Rover's Dave Challinor.

His form with Birmingham was such that he won four full caps for Wales, the first against Switzerland in 1996. However, in 1997-98 he failed to agree terms with the Midlands club and after a loan spell at Ipswich Town, he joined Reading in February 1998 for a fee of £75,000.

LEWIS, DAI

Outside-left Dai Lewis joined the Swans in 1929 and after impressing in the club's reserve team he was given his first team debut during the course of the 1930-31 season. The following campaign saw Lewis a virtual ever-present in the Swansea side as they finished the season in 15th place in the Second Division. That 1931-32 campaign was Lewis' best during six seasons with the Swans as he won a Welsh Cup winners' medal following a 2-0 win over Wrexham.

His performances led to him winning international recognition for Wales and in October 1932 he played his first game for his country against Scotland in Edinburgh. His wizardry on the wing, laying on three of Wales' goals in a 5-2 win. Lewis won a second cap against England at Wrexham a month later in a match which ended goalless but he was never given a further opportunity to represent his country.

He went on to score five goals for Swansea in 109 league games before leaving the club at the end of the 1935-36 season.

LEWIS, DUDLEY

Welsh Schoolboy international Dudley Lewis became an apprentice at the Vetch Field before turning professional some six months later. Swans' manager John Toshack gave the central defender his first team debut in the

Dudley Lewis

1980-81 season at Notts County. After returning to the club's reserve side, he was restored to the first team as sweeper for the visit of Bolton Wanderers, a match which the Swans won 3-0. He then had an outstanding game at Deepdale as the Welsh side beat Preston North End 3-1 to clinch promotion to the First Division.

He soon established himself at the heart of the Swansea defence and over the next nine seasons went on to appear in 230 league games. His performances during that period unbelievably earned him just one Welsh cap when he came on as a substitute in a 1-1 draw against Brazil at Ninian Park.

Lewis left Vetch Field in the summer of 1989 to play for Huddersfield Town but after 34 appearances and a loan spell at Halifax Town, he ended his league career with Wrexham, being released at the end of the 1991-92 season.

LEWIS, WILF

Despite only playing a handful of games for the Swansea first team, Wilf Lewis made his international debut for Wales against England in 1927, starring in a 3-3 draw. This followed his first hat-trick for the club which came in a 3-0 home win over Oldham Athletic on 27 December 1926. Lewis netted a second hat-trick for the Swans on 1 October 1927 as they beat South Shields 6-3 in a match in which they were always behind until the last quarter of an hour! He ended that season as the club's top scorer as they finished sixth in Division Two, netting 25 goals in 39 games.

His form was such that he attracted a lot of attention from the top clubs, and it came as no surprise in November 1928 when he joined Huddersfield Town for £6,500, the highest fee that the Swans had received for a player at that time.

After leaving Leeds Road he joined Derby County where he was one of five players tried at inside-forward during the 1931-32 season and though he scored three goals in eight games, he was released and joined non-league Yeovil Town. Lewis who won six caps for his country scored a remarkable 43 goals in just 64 league games for Swansea.

LEYLAND DAF CUP

The Leyland Daf Cup replaced the Sherpa Van Trophy for the 1989-90 season. After losing their first match in the competition 2-1 at Bristol City, the Swans lost their second group match at home to Reading by a similar scoreline and so failed to qualify for the knockout stages.

In 1990-91 the Swans drew both of their group games, against Torquay United (Away) and Shrewsbury Town (Home) 1-1, which necessitated a play-off game against the Gay Meadow club to determine which side went through to the knockout stages. Two goals apiece from Andy Legg and Jimmy Gilligan gave the Swans a 4-2 win and a first round tie away to Birmingham City. Unfortunately after a superb defensive display which resulted in a goalless draw, the Swans went out of the competition 4-2 on penalties.

LONGEST LEAGUE RUNS

Of undefeated matches	19	1970-71
Of undefeated home matches	28	1925-27
Of league wins	8	1961
Of league defeats	9	1990-91
Of home wins	17	1948-49
Of away wins	4	1955-56, 1987-88, 1993
Of league matches without a win	15	1989
Of undefeated away matches	12	1970-71
Without a home win	9	1938
Without an away win	46	1982-84

LOWEST
The lowest number of goals scored by Swansea in a single league season is 36 in 1983-84 when the club finished 21st in the Second Division and were relegated.

The club's lowest points record in the league occurred in seasons 1946-47 and 1983-84 when the Swans gained just 29 points and on each occasion were relegated.

LUCAS, BILLY
Billy Lucas began his league career with Swindon Town and had just established himself in their first team when war broke out and interrupted his career. He had compensations, as he played in several wartime and two Victory internationals for Wales. When the hostilities ended he resumed his career with Swindon.

In March 1948, Swansea manager Bill McCandless paid a club record transfer fee of £11,000 to bring Lucas to the Vetch Field as the missing link in a side that would claim the Third Division (South) Championship the following season.

His early displays for the Swans led to him winning the first of seven full caps for Wales when in October 1948 he played against Scotland at Ninian Park. Able to play at both wing-half and inside-forward, he went on to score 35 goals in 203 league games for the Swans before leaving the Vetch in December 1953 to become player-manager of Newport County. The value of his leadership qualities were only really noticed when he left the club.

At Somerton Park, Lucas was in charge of one of the smallest squads in the Football League and had to sell to survive. He resigned his post in April 1961 but was re-appointed less than a year later when Bobby Evans was sacked.

In February 1967 he returned to the Vetch as manager but the Swans were struggling to avoid relegation from the Third Division. Unfortunately he was unable to save them but he was instrumental in bringing in a good number of young players to the club.

He resigned in March 1969 but returned to Somerton Park for a third spell, and in the first six months of this period worked without wages. In 1972-73 County missed out on promotion on goal average but Lucas who later became the club's general manager left in 1975 to spend more time on his business.

M

MAHONEY, JOHN

Though he was born in Cardiff, John Mahoney's father was a rugby play-er who moved north to become a rugby league professional and so he started his football at Ashton United before moving to Crewe Alexandra.

He later joined Stoke City where the coaching staff worked on his initial

John Mahoney

ungainly style and turned him into a fine midfielder who won 51 caps for Wales. The first of these came against England in 1968 and his last against the same country some 15 years later.

At Stoke he won a Football League Cup winners' medal in 1972 and went on to score 25 goals in 284 league games before joining Middlesbrough for a fee of £90,000. After two seasons at Ayresome Park he linked up with his cousin John Toshack at Swansea and played a major role in the Welsh club's renaissance.

His first game in Swansea colours came in a 4-1 League Cup win over Bournemouth and despite a series of niggling injuries during his first few weeks with the club, he soon settled down. In 1980-81 he won a Welsh Cup winners' medal and helped the club win promotion to the First Division. He was outstanding as the Swans played top flight football for the first time in their history.

He had appeared in 110 league games for the Vetch Field club when in March 1983 a broken leg against Brighton ended his playing career.

After a spell on Swansea's commercial staff, he went into management with Bangor City and took them into Europe. He later managed Newport County until the Somerton Park club were wound up before returning to take charge at Bangor for a second time.

MANAGERS

This is the complete list of Swansea's full-time managers with the inclusive dates during which they held office:

Walter Whittaker	1912-1914	John Toshack	1978-1983
John Bartlett	1914-1915	Colin Appleton	1984
Joe Bradshaw	1919-1926	John Bond	1984-1985
Jimmy Thompson	1927-1931	Tommy Hutchison	1985-1986
Neil Harris	1934-1939	Terry Yorath	1986-1989
Haydn Green	1939-1947	Ian Evans	1989-1990
Billy McCandless	1947-1955	Terry Yorath	1990-1991
Ron Burgess	1955-1958	Frank Burrows	1991-1995
Trevor Morris	1958-1965	Keith Cullis	1996
Glyn Davies	1965-1966	Jan Molby	1996-1997
Billy Lucas	1967-1969	Micky Adams	1997
Roy Bentley	1969-1972	Alan Cork	1997-1998
Harry Gregg	1972-1975	John Hollins	1998-
Harry Griffiths	1975-1977		

MARATHON MATCHES

Swansea have been involved in two FA Cup matches that have gone to three matches. These were against West Ham United in a first round tie in 1921-22 and against Crystal Palace in a third round match in 1979-80. On both occasions the Swans won through to the next round at the third attempt.

MARKSMEN - LEAGUE

Swansea's top league goalscorer is Ivor Allchurch who struck 166 league goals during his two spells with the club:

1.	Ivor Allchurch	166
2.	Robbie James	115
3.	Herbie Williams	102
4.	Jack Fowler	100
5.	Alan Curtis	95
6.	Harry Deacon	88
7.	Len Thompson	86
8.	Keith Todd	76
9.	Harry Griffiths	71
10.	Mel Charles	69

Though Ivor Allchurch has scored most league goals for the Swans, Jack Fowler is the top marksman as far as goals per game are concerned (0.60), though to be fair, he was an out-and-out striker, whilst Ivor made many goals for his colleagues as a 'scheming inside-forward'. It must also be said that Mel Charles, Robbie James and Harry Griffiths would probably have scored more goals if they had played up front all the time, Griffiths in fact played many of his games at left-back!

MARTIN, TUDOR

Tudor Martin began his career with Bridgend Town before joining West Bromwich Albion. After four years at the Hawthorns he signed for Newport County and was capped at full international level for Wales against Ireland. He only spent one season at Somerton Park, scoring 34 goals in 27 Third Division (South) matches and so attracting the attention of Major Frank Buckley, manager of Wolverhampton Wanderers.

At Molineux he scored nine goals in 15 games in a two year period with the club, but netted 60 goals in Wolves' Central League championship-winning season of 1931-32.

Martin then joined Swansea and in his first four games scored three goals before being injured. He soon returned to full fitness and in January 1933 netted his first hat-trick for the club against Fulham. The following season his progress with the Welsh club was hampered by a series of injuries before he was recalled to the side and scored his second hat-trick against West Ham United. In 1935-36, Martin scored all four goals in the defeat of Bury but at the end of the season he was allowed to leave the Vetch Field after scoring 55 goals in 116 games.

He then joined West Ham United and made a sensational debut for the Hammers, scoring a hat-trick as the London club were beaten 5-3 at Newcastle United. Yet after just 11 games for West Ham, he left to join Southend United where he ended his career.

MARUSTIK, CHRIS
The son of a Czech immigrant, Chris Marustik caught the eye of Harry Griffiths whilst playing for Swansea Schoolboys. Signed on as an apprentice at the Vetch, he later turned professional and made his debut as a substitute in the second round of the League Cup as the Swans drew 2-2 at home to Tottenham Hotspur in August 1978. His full league debut didn't come until seven months later when the Swans were beaten 2-0 at Peterborough United.

Chris Marustik

Quick and versatile, his talent was nurtured by John Toshack, John Mahoney and Les Chappell, and over the next six seasons he went on to score 11 goals in 153 games before leaving to join Cardiff City in October 1985.

Injuries hampered his progress at Ninian Park and after making 43 league appearances in two years with the Bluebirds, he left to play non-league football for Barry Town.

MATCH OF THE DAY

Swansea City's first appearance on BBC's 'Match of the Day' was on 5 May 1979 when they drew 2-2 at Plymouth Argyle. City's scorers that day were Alan Curtis and John Toshack.

MAY, EDDIE

Eddie May began his career as a centre-forward with Athenian League club Dagenham before a switch to full-back alerted Southend United manager Ted Fenton, who gave him a chance with the Roots Hall club. It was the former West Ham boss who moved May to centre-half and he went on to appear in 111 league games before joining Wrexham for £5,000 in the summer of 1968.

Over the next nine seasons, May missed very few matches for the Robins and was ever-present in seasons 1971-72 and 1975-76. During the club's promotion-winning season of 1969-70, May scored seven league goals from his position at centre-half. It was his best return - the Robins being undefeated whenever he scored!

Captain for most of his time at the Racecourse Ground, he led the Robins to the sixth round of the FA Cup in 1973-74 and to the quarter-finals of the European Cup Winners' Cup in 1975-76. At the end of that season, May, who had played in 410 first team games, scoring 44 goals, joined Swansea on a free transfer.

The 33-year-old defender added experience to the Swansea defence and was soon elected captain in place of George Smith. A virtual ever-present in his time at the Vetch Field, May scored six goals in 90 games including one in the 4-4 home draw with Stockport County on 22 March 1977 when the Swans were 4-0 down shortly after half-time.

On leaving Swansea, he took up coaching posts with Leicester City and Charlton Athletic. After managing Newport County who had just lost their league status, he was in charge of Cardiff City from 1991 to 1994 before becoming boss of Torquay United.

McCANDLESS, BILLY

One of the great characters of the game, Billy McCandless had the unique record of having taken three separate South Wales sides to the Third Division (South) Championship.

He played in three Irish Cup Finals for Linfield before moving to Ibrox Park where he gained seven League Championship medals in Rangers' great side of that time. McCandless won nine caps for Ireland, winning his first against England in a 1-1 draw in Belfast in October 1919. He left Rangers in the close season of 1930 to become the player-manager of Ballymena United. In 1934 he became the manager of Dundee but three years later he took charge of Newport County.

He inherited some excellent players and soon developed them into an outstanding combination, guiding them to the Third Division (South) Championship in 1938-39. Unfortunately, the war years decimated the Newport County side and Somerton Park was requisitioned by the Army during the hostilities and the club had to close down. In April 1946 McCandless resigned, but two months later he became manager of Cardiff City, replacing Cyril Spiers.

In his first season at Ninian Park the Bluebirds won the Third Division (South) Championship, finishing seven points clear of their nearest rivals Queen's Park Rangers.

In November 1947 McCandless left Cardiff for Swansea and breathed life back into a failing Vetch Field side and led them to fifth place in his first season. In 1948-49 the crowds flocked to the Vetch as the team produced some exciting football, eventually winning the Third Division (South) Championship. Their 62 points put them seven points ahead of Reading and their joy was complete when they finished the following season two places above Cardiff City in the Second Division. McCandless died in 1955 but he left behind a wealth of talent including the Allchurch brothers, Mel Charles, Cliff Jones and Terry Medwin.

McCARTHY, SEAN

A keen supporter of the Swans as a youngster, Sean McCarthy realised an ambition when he signed professional forms for the Vetch Field club in October 1985 after playing for his home-town club Bridgend Town in the Welsh League.

The powerful striker made his debut in a 1-1 home draw against Chesterfield the following month and over the next three seasons proved himself a handful for opposition defences. He had scored 38 goals in 113 first team games when he left Swansea in the summer of 1988 to join Plymouth Argyle for £50,000. In two seasons at Home Park, McCarthy scored 26 goals in 81 games before leaving to sign for Bradford City for a fee of £250,000.

His form at Valley Parade was such that he won 'B' international honours for Wales and top scored in each of his three seasons with the club. He had found the net 79 times in 160 first team outings for the Bantams when in December 1993 he moved to Oldham Athletic for £500,000.

In his early days at Boundary Park he lost his goalscoring touch and suffered from a series of niggling injuries. He also had a loan spell at Bristol City but is now back with Oldham hoping to add to his total of 46 goals in the 161 appearances he has made for the club.

McCRORY, SAM

Belfast-born centre-forward Sam McCrory began his footballing career with Linfield before Swansea brought him into league football. McCrory made his debut for the Swans on 3 October 1946 against Southampton.

Over the next four seasons he proved himself a prolific goalscorer and in February 1949 he netted a hat-trick in a 6-1 home win over Torquay United. That season the Swans won the Third Division (South) Championship but towards the end of the following campaign he joined Ipswich Town with full-back Jim Feeney for a combined fee of £10,500.

After making his debut in the East Anglian derby at Norwich's Carrow Road, McCrory had the dubious distinction of becoming the first Ipswich player to be sent-off since the club joined the Football League in a 5-0 defeat at Aldershot. In 1950-51 he was the club's top scorer with 21 league goals including a hat-trick in a 3-1 win over Crystal Palace. He headed the scoring charts again the following season with 16 goals but in the summer of 1952 he joined newly promoted Plymouth Argyle.

Never an automatic choice at Home Park, his career was revived somewhat after his transfer to Southend United in 1955 and at the age of 33, he received his sole international cap for Northern Ireland, scoring in a rare win over England in 1957.

McLAUGHLIN, JIMMY

After failing to make the grade with Birmingham City, Derry-born winger Jimmy McLaughlin joined Shrewsbury Town in the summer of 1960. His form for the Gay Meadow club was such that two years later he won the first of 12 full caps for Northern Ireland when he played against England in a 3-1 defeat at Belfast.

In May 1963 McLaughlin, who had scored 100 goals in 340 League and Cup games including a hat-trick in a 7-2 defeat of Bristol Rovers when Frank Clarke also netted three goals, joined Swansea for £16,000.

He made his debut in the opening game of the 1963-64 season when the Swans drew 1-1 with Grimsby Town. During his first season at the Vetch, McLaughlin played an important part in the club's run to the FA Cup semi-finals, scoring some vital goals - the second in the 2-0 fifth round replay win over Stoke City and the opening goal in the Welsh club's 2-1 win over Liverpool at Anfield in the following round. On 23 November 1965, McLaughlin netted his only hat-trick for the club in a 5-0 win over Bournemouth, but in March 1967 after he had scored 45 goals in 123 games he left to join Football League newcomers Peterborough United.

After just eight league appearances for 'The Posh' he returned to Shrewsbury but in November 1972 he rejoined Swansea as player-coach. He went on to score 47 goals in 151 league games for the Swans before hanging up his boots.

McPHERSON, LACHLAN
Lachlan McPherson joined the Swans from Notts County in the summer of 1924 and in his first season with the club won a Third Division (South) Championship medal as the Vetch Field club lifted the title, finishing one point ahead of runners-up Plymouth Argyle.

In his early days with the club, the Scottish-born half-back was often accused of 'doing too much' on the ball but when the Swans beat First Division Arsenal 2-1 in the FA Cup quarter-final of 1925-26, it was McPherson who did a superb man-to-man marking job on the great Charlie Buchan.

At the start of the 1927-28 season, McPherson was given a more adventurous role and responded by scoring hat-tricks in successive home matches as Manchester City were beaten 5-3 and Wolverhampton Wanderers 6-0. Not surprisingly, McPherson's form at this time led to a number of clubs making inquiries about the talented Scot and there were strong rumours that he was about to sign for Huddersfield Town. However, he stayed at the Vetch for another season and had scored 30 goals in 199 league games when along with Ben Williams he joined Everton.

On his first return to the Vetch Field with Everton on 3 January 1931, McPherson was outstanding in a 5-2 win for the Goodison Park club. He went on to play in 31 games for the Toffees before joining New Brighton in August 1932, where he later ended his career.

MEDWIN, TERRY

Terry Medwin spent most of his childhood at Swansea Prison where his father was a prison officer. His talents were recognised at an early age and he won schoolboy international honours for Wales. The goalscoring winger began to attract a great deal of attention from a number of First Division clubs but when Swansea offered him the chance to sign as a part-time professional in 1949, he readily accepted.

After a few seasons of reserve team football, he was given his first team debut against Doncaster Rovers in January 1952. He scored in the opening minute of the match and though the Swans lost, he kept his place for the remainder of the season, alternating between the right-wing and centre-forward.

His performances for the Vetch Field club led to him winning his first full cap when he played for Wales against Northern Ireland in Belfast in April 1953.

After finishing as the Swans' top scorer in 1955-56, Medwin realised that his future lay at another club and so in April 1956 after scoring 59 goals in 148 league games he joined Tottenham Hotspur for £18,000.

He made his Spurs' debut on the opening day of the 1956-57 season, scoring twice in a 4-1 defeat of Preston North End and in October of that season he was back in the Welsh side to play Scotland. He won 29 caps for his country, all but the first three with the White Hart Lane club. He was occasionally played at centre-forward, the role in which he struck four times in the 6-0 home defeat of Leicester City in April 1959. A Tottenham regular for four seasons, he was unfortunate to lose his place to Terry Dyson in the 1960-61 'double' season, although he played in 15 League and FA Cup games as deputy for either Dyson or Cliff Jones. He gained some consolation in 1962 when he was a member of the Spurs side that retained the FA Cup.

His career was wrecked when he sustained a broken leg on the 1963 tour of South Africa and though he tried to make a comeback he had to abandon his efforts. He later returned to the professional game by coaching at Cardiff, Fulham and Norwich City before becoming assistant-manager to John Toshack at Swansea, as the side reached the First Division. Sadly in 1983, ill health forced him to retire from an active participation with the club.

MELVILLE, ANDY

Swansea-born Andy Melville began his career with his home-town club and progressed from the youth training scheme to make his senior debut as a substitute in a 3-1 home defeat by Bristol City in November 1985. In his early days with the Swans there was something of a problem in that his best position was not readily apparent. He was tried in most positions before settling into the back four. He won a permanent place in the Swansea side in 1986-87 and helped the Welsh club win promotion the following season.

He was appointed Swansea captain at the age of 20 but in July 1990 after scoring 29 goals in 213 games for the Vetch Field club, he joined Oxford United for £275,000, plus a percentage of any future transfer fee. In three seasons at the Manor Ground, he appeared in 159 games before being transferred to Sunderland in the summer of 1993.

The Welsh international who has won 32 caps for his country made a disastrous debut for the Wearsiders in a 5-0 defeat at Derby County on the opening day of the 1993-94 season. His first three seasons at Roker Park were spent in relegation battles but in 1995-96, Melville played in 40 league games as the Wearsiders won the First Division Championship.

Powerful in the air and always dangerous at set pieces, he acquitted himself well in the Premiership. A broken nose ruled him out of the last seven games of the season when his experience could have helped the club in their attempt to avoid the drop.

An injury ended his virtual monopoly of a back-four position but after a loan spell at Bradford City, he returned to Sunderland and helped them win the First Division Championship.

MILLINGTON, TONY

Welsh international goalkeeper Tony Millington began his career with West Bromwich Albion and made 40 league appearances for the Baggies before joining Crystal Palace in October 1964.

The Hawarden-born 'keeper failed to establish himself with the Selhurst Park club and in March 1966 signed for Peterborough United. Millington went on to appear in 118 league games for 'The Posh' and set the club record for international caps whilst he was with them, a record he still holds today. He joined Swansea in the summer of 1969 and made his debut in a goalless draw at home to Chesterfield on the opening day of the club's Fourth Division promotion-winning season of 1969-70, a campaign in which he kept 20 clean sheets.

A brave and agile goalkeeper, Millington had very few bad games during his five seasons at Vetch Field and his performances won him a further eight full caps. During the 1971-72 season, Millington equalled Jack Parry's record sequence of remaining unbeaten in five consecutive games, a record that was broken by Dai Davies in 1981-82. A great Vetch Field favourite, Tony Millington appeared in 178 league games for the Swans.

MILNE, WILF

Wilf Milne is the club record holder for the greatest number of appearances in a Swansea shirt, having played in 657 first team games between 1920 and 1937.

He played in the club's first ever Football League game when they lost 3-0 at Portsmouth on 28 August 1920 and was a member of the Swansea side which won the Third Division (South) Championship in 1924-25. The following season Milne played his part in the club's run to the FA Cups semi-finals where after beating Arsenal in the sixth round, they lost 3-0 to the eventual winners, Bolton Wanderers.

Famous for his sliding tackle, Milne went on to make club history with a record 585 league appearances. He scored his first goal for the Swans in his 501st league match - from the penalty spot - and then added another in the final match of the 1933-34 season - had he missed, the Vetch Field side would have been relegated!

In 1936-37 when the Swans were travelling to play Leicester City at Filbert Street, the club's 'keeper Moore had a swollen knee and was unable to play. The only available replacement was Wilf Milne - in his 17th season with the club - he performed heroics and kept a clean sheet in a goalless draw. Because the club were playing two games in three days in the Midlands, Milne kept his place for the next match but the Vetch Field side lost 6-1!

Milne left the Vetch at the end of that season but not before a special benefit match had been played on behalf of this loyal servant.

MOLBY, JAN

Danish international Jan Molby joined Liverpool in the summer of 1984 for a fee of £575,000 after a successful period at with Dutch side Ajax of Amsterdam. His influence in the midfield minimised the loss of Graeme Souness to Italian soccer, though he was later used as a sweeper. He was a virtual ever-present in 1985-86 when Liverpool did the 'double', winning the League Championship and beating Everton 3-1 in the FA Cup Final. Though he won a second League Championship medal in 1989-90, he began to suffer from injuries and lost his place in the Liverpool side. Despite competition from Ronnie Whelan and Steve McMahon, he went on to score 61 goals in 292 games before spells on loan with Barnsley and Norwich City. He then joined Swansea as player-manager.

He made his debut for the Swans in a goalless draw at York City in February 1996 and though the Vetch Field club were relegated to the Third

Jan Molby

Division, Molby's international class stood out. In 1996-97 he scored some vital goals as he led the Swans to the play-offs and as well as winning a Manager of the Month award, he was also included in the Third Division PFA side.

Molby, who believed in playing quality football, introduced a number of good youngsters but with little cash available, the results started to go against the Swans, and on 7 October 1997 after just one win in eight league games, he was sacked.

MORRIS, TREVOR
After a spell with Ipswich Town, he 'guested' for Cardiff City during the Second World War but his playing career was ended by a broken leg in a game against Bristol City during December 1941.

During the war years, Morris piloted the lead aircraft of a squadron of Lancaster bombers on D-Day and flew in more than 40 missions over enemy territory for which he was awarded the Distinguished Flying Medal.

He joined Cardiff City as assistant-secretary in 1946 but following Cyril Spiers' resignation, he was appointed secretary-manager. Cardiff were relegated from the First Division in 1957 and a year later, he left Ninian Park to work as general manager with Swansea Town.

Morris was in charge at the Vetch for seven years during which time he took the Swans to the FA Cup semi-final in 1964. A year after the success, the Vetch Field club were relegated to the Third Division and Morris resigned from his position. He had a brief spell in charge of Newport County before being appointed secretary of the Welsh FA, a position he held for 11 years.

MOST GOALS IN A SEASON
Swansea scored 92 goals in 46 Division Four matches during the 1976-77 season when they finished fifth. Victories at the Vetch Field included Brentford (5-3), Workington '4-0), Hartlepool United (4-2), Aldershot (4-2), and Torquay United (4-1), whilst the game against Stockport County ended all-square at 4-4. Jeremy Charles in his first season with the club netted 20 league goals.

MOST MATCHES
Swansea played their most number of matches, 66, in 1993-94 season. This comprised 46 league games, two FA Cup games, four Football League Cup games, nine Autoglass Trophy games and five Welsh Cup games.

N

NAME CHANGE
On 24 February 1970 during the club's Fourth Division promotion-winning season, the Vetch Field side changed its name from Swansea Town to Swansea City with the elevation of the town to city status.

NEUTRAL GROUNDS
The club's FA Cup semi-finals were played on neutral grounds - White Hart Lane in 1926 and Villa Park in 1964 - and the club's FA Cup first round second replay against West Ham United in 1921-22 was played at Bristol City's Ashton Gate.

A number of the club's appearances in the Welsh Cup Final were played at neutral grounds - Mid Rhondda, Ninian Park and Shrewsbury, whilst the club's success in the Autoglass Trophy Final at Wembley also qualifies for inclusion.

NICHOLAS, DAI
Dai Nicholas played for the Swans as an amateur in the years leading up to the First World War before joining Merthyr Town. He later played for Stoke where he was capped at full international level for Wales in the match against Scotland in 1923. He was transferred to Swansea in November 1924 and made his debut at inside-left in the match against Bournemouth and over the next six seasons, appeared regularly in the Vetch Field side.

Though he scored some spectacular goals for Swansea, Nicholas was more of a provider, and in the FA Cup fifth round match of 1925-26 against Millwall it was he that provided Fowler with the opportunity to score three minutes from time and take the club through to the quarter-final where they met Arsenal. In that sixth round tie, Nicholas' pass split the Gunners' defence wide open and allowed Thompson to race onto the ball and score the opening goal in the famous victory over the Highbury club.

In 1927 Nicholas added two more caps to his collection when he played against England and Northern Ireland but left the club at the end of the 1929-30 season having scored 13 goals in 150 games.

NICHOLAS, JACK

After beginning his career with his home-town club Staines, Jack Nicholas joined Derby County and took over the right-back position when Jimmy Methven became the Rams' manager in 1906. Nicholas who appeared in 143 games for County, stayed at the Baseball Ground until the emergence of Jack Atkin and then moved to Swansea.

Nicholas was made the Swans' captain in their first year as a professional club and kept the role which he performed to great effect throughout the club's pre-First World War Southern League days. Despite his efforts, the Swans who came close to promotion in each of the three seasons he skippered the side, failed to achieve their goal.

He returned to the Vetch Field after the hostilities as player-coach and it was whilst in that capacity that he had the misfortune to discover the body of 'Tich' Evans who had taken his own life, lying under the Main Stand.

A popular figure at the Vetch and a very skilful footballer, he was the father of Derby County's FA Cup winning captain.

NICKNAMES

The club's nickname is the 'Swans'. The Cambrian Daily Leader on Monday 14 April 1913 referred to 'the Swans' well-earned victory' playing their first match at Morriston on Saturday 31 August 1912.

NON-LEAGUE

'Non-League' is the shorthand term for clubs which are not members of the Football League. The club's record against non-league opposition in the FA Cup is as follows:

Date	Opponents	Stage	Venue	Score
26.11.1966	Folkestone	Rd 1	Away	2-2
29.11.1966	Folkestone	Rd 1 R	Home	7-2
05.12.1966	Nuneaton Borough	Rd 2	Away	0-2
18.12.1967	Enfield	Rd 1	Home	2-0
16.11.1968	Oxford City	Rd 1	Away	3-2
07.12.1968	Weymouth	Rd 2	Away	1-1
10.12.1968	Weymouth	Rd 2 R	Home	2-0
15.11.1969	Kettering	Rd 1	Away	2-0
06.12.1969	Oxford City	Rd 2	Away	5-1
21.11.1970	Telford United	Rd 2	Home	6-2
02.01.1971	Rhyl	Rd 3	Home	6-1
18.11.1972	Margate	Rd 1	Away	0-1
23.11.1974	Kettering	Rd 1	Home	1-1
26.11.1974	Kettering	Rd 1 R	Away	1-3
20.11.1976	Minehead	Rd 1	Home	0-1
26.11.1977	Leatherhead	Rd 1	Away	0-0
29.11.1977	Leatherhead	Rd 1 R	Home	2-1
25.11.1978	Hillingdon Borough	Rd 1	Home	4-1
16.12.1978	Woking	Rd 2	Home	2-2
20.11.1978	Woking	Rd 2 R	Away	5-3
17.11.1984	Bognor Regis	Rd 1	Home	1-1
21.11.1984	Bognor Regis	Rd 1 R	Away	1-3
16.11.1985	Leyton Wealdstone	Rd 1	Home	2-0
15.11.1986	Wealdstone	Rd 1	Away	1-1
18.11.1986	Wealdstone	Rd 1 R	Home	4-1
24.11.1986	Slough	Rd 2	Home	3-0
14.11.1987	Hayes	Rd 1	Away	1-0
18.11.1989	Kidderminster H.	Rd 1	Away	3-2
17.11.1990	Welling United	Rd 1	Home	5-2
13.11.1993	Nuneaton Borough	Rd 1	Home	1-1
23.11.1993	Nuneaton Borough	Rd 1 R	Away	1-2
21.11.1994	Walton and Hersham	Rd 1	Away	2-0
04.12.1994	Bashley	Rd 2	Away	1-0

NUMBERING

When Swansea entertained West Bromwich Albion at the Vetch Field on the opening day of the 1939-40 season, it was the first time that the clubs had been required to number their players in a prescribed manner.

NURSE, MEL

Welsh Schoolboy international centre-half Mel Nurse was linked to his home-town club via the juniors and signed professional forms for the Swans in June 1955. Over the next seven seasons, Nurse gave many outstanding performances in the heart of the Swansea defence and in 1960 after winning two Welsh Under-23 caps, he made his full international debut against England at Wembley. It was the first of 12 full caps for his country, nine of them whilst with the Swans.

Nurse did not score many goals but when he did they were usually spectacular efforts and perhaps none more so than his 30-yard thunderbolt against Burnley in an FA Cup fourth round replay at Turf Moor which the Swans lost after holding their First Division opponents to a goalless draw at the Vetch. Towards the end of that season, Mel Nurse captained Swansea for the first time and proved himself to be an inspirational leader. However, as the club struggled in the lower reaches of the Second Division, Nurse requested a transfer on a number of occasions, all of which were turned down.

Eventually the Swans had to release him and in September 1962, he joined Middlesbrough for a fee of £25,000. A commanding figure in the 'Boro defence, he was soon appointed captain and was a virtual ever-present in his three seasons at Ayresome Park. One of his biggest regrets must have been scoring the goal which sent the Vetch Field club crashing into the Third Division.

Nurse's wife wanted to return nearer to South Wales and in the summer of 1965 he joined Swindon Town for £15,000. He spent three seasons at the County Ground before renewing his association with Swansea in June 1968.

He went on to score 11 goals in 256 league games in his two spells with the club before entering non-league football with Suffolk club Bury before finishing his career with Merthyr Tydfil, for whom he was playing when he suffered a broken leg.

O'DRISCOLL, JACK

Outside-right Jack O'Driscoll joined Swansea from Cork for a fee of £3,000 in July 1947 and impressed in his first season with the club. Possessing great pace and a powerful shot, O'Driscoll's crosses provided Richards and McCrory with goal opportunities in 1948-49 as the club won the Third Division (South) Championship. During this season, O'Driscoll was capped on six occasions - making three appearances for Northern Ireland and three for the Republic of Ireland.

Inevitably his performances for both club and country attracted the attention of the bigger clubs but just when it seemed as if he would move on to the top flight, he badly damaged an ankle which was to end his league career. At the end of the 1951-52 season after which he had scored 26 goals including a number of last minute winners in 147 games, he left to play for Llanelli who were then playing in the Southern League.

OLDEST PLAYER

The oldest player to line up in a Swansea first team is Tommy Hutchison. He was 43 years 171 days old when he played his last game for the club against Southend United (Home 1-4) on 12 March 1991.

OVERSEAS PLAYERS

Yugoslav Dzemal Hadziabdic was the first overseas player to be imported by the Welsh club when he joined the Swans from Velez Mostar in August

1980 and made his debut in a 3-1 League Cup defeat at Arsenal on 2 September 1980. The popular full-back who was commonly known as 'Jimmy' went on to play in 89 league games for the Swans.

Yugoslav defender Ante Rajkovic joined the Vetch Field club from Sarajevo in March 1981 and played his first game in a goalless draw against Bristol City. An important member of the Swansea side when the Welsh club arrived in the First Division, he appeared in 80 league games before leaving the Vetch.

Danish international Jan Molby, who appeared in 67 matches for his country, joined Swansea as player-manager in February 1996 but after 44 first team appearances was sacked in October 1997 following a dismal run of results.

Left-sided defender Joao Moreira joined the Swans from Portuguese club Benfica for £50,000 in the summer of 1996 but after appearing in 25 games was given a free transfer by Alan Cork in March 1998.

The Swans have had a number of players with foreign-sounding surnames on their books including Kwame Ampadu and Chris Marustik but both were born in the British Isles!

OWN GOALS

The first own goal in a game involving Swansea occurred in the semi-final of the 1912-13 Welsh Cup against Cardiff City at Ninian Park. The Swans won 4-2 with Cassidy of Cardiff putting through his own goal to register the first-ever goal of that category for the Vetch Field club.

P

PALMER, DES

Though he had a goal ratio of almost one goal every other game, Des Palmer, who made his debut against Hull City in September 1952, never established himself as a first team regular in his seven seasons at the Vetch Field.

After making his international debut for Wales against Czechoslovakia in 1957, he scored a hat-trick in only his second full international as the Welsh beat East Germany 4-1 to show the Swansea board what they were missing, ending the 1956-57 season as the club's top scorer with 18 goals in 30 games. Though he never netted a hat-trick for the Swans, he did score 38 goals in 83 league games before leaving the club in March 1959 to join Liverpool in return for £4,000 and wing-half Ron Saunders.

Sadly for Palmer, his move to Liverpool turned into a disaster when he suffered knee ligament damage. After leaving Anfield he played in South Africa before Derby County manager Harry Storer took a gamble on him and signed Palmer for the Rams, but the move didn't work out.

PARRY, JACK

Goalkeeper Jack Parry joined the Swans from local team Clydach in September 1946 and made his league bow during 1946-47, the first season of league football after the Second World War. Over the next five seasons, he went on to appear in 99 league games, winning a Third Division (South) Championship medal in 1948-49 when he appeared in 22 games.

He earned a reputation for being a brave and agile goalkeeper, never afraid to dive at an opponent's feet. His performances for the Swans led to him winning a full cap for Wales when he played in the game against Scotland at Ninian Park in October 1950 in a match the Welsh lost 3-1.

Parry left the Vetch in August 1951 and joined Ipswich Town. He was the Portman Road club's first-choice 'keeper for four seasons, appearing in 138 league games and winning a Third Division (South) Championship medal in 1953-54.

PASCOE, COLIN

Colin Pascoe joined Swansea as a 16-year-old apprentice in 1981 when the Vetch Field club were members of the First Division of the Football League. After making his debut as a substitute for the injured John Mahoney against Brighton in March 1983, he played his first full game against Liverpool at Anfield.

During his first season with the Swans, he represented the Welsh Youth side and in 1983-84 he was chosen for the Welsh Under-21 side on four

Colin Pascoe

occasions. Two years after winning his Welsh Youth cap he was selected for the Wales senior side against Norway. Pascoe had played in 201 first team games for the Swans when he was transferred to Sunderland for £70,000 in March 1998.

After scoring the Wearsiders' goal in a 2-1 defeat at York City on his debut, Pascoe netted the winner against Chesterfield in a 3-2 win for Sunderland. He also scored in his third game for the north-east club in a 4-1 win at Southend United. He helped Sunderland reach the First Division via the 1989-90 play-offs even though it was at the expense of Swindon Town who were found guilty of financial irregularities and relegated from the top flight. Pascoe went on to score 26 goals in 151 games before returning to Swansea for £120,000 after a loan spell with the Vetch Field club. He took his total of goals for the Swans to 67 in 324 League and Cup games before being released by the club after suffering damage to his ankle ligaments.

PAUL, ROY

A native of the Rhondda, Roy Paul's first taste of senior soccer came in 1939 in a wartime league game for Swansea and when football resumed after the hostilities, he was a member of the Vetch Field's side which won the Third Division (South) title in 1948-49.

Roy Paul

Paul also looked with interest at the situation in Colombia when other British players like Neil Franklin and Charlie Mitten went to Bogota in search of soccer fortune, but within a couple of weeks of arriving in South America, he was back in South Wales 'thoroughly disgusted with the situation'. The Swansea directors immediately placed him on the transfer list and two weeks later, Paul, who had scored 14 goals in 160 games, joined Manchester City for £18,000.

When the Maine Road club won promotion to the First Division in 1950-51, Paul was a star performer, missing only one game and scoring three goals, two of them coming in the 3-1 home win over Birmingham City on Christmas Day. Some six years later he captained Manchester City to success in the FA Cup Final in another 3-1 victory over the Midlands side, twelve months after he had collected a losers' medal against Newcastle United.

The winner of 33 Welsh caps, nine whilst with the Swans, he joined Worcester City in June 1957 as their player-manager.

PEARCE, CYRIL
Centre-forward Cyril Pearce joined Swansea from Newport County and in 1931-32, his first season with the club, wrote his name into the record books. He netted hat-tricks in successive games in the space of three days, scoring four against Notts County at the Vetch and three at Port Vale two days later. He had scored 17 goals in the opening 13 games of the season and despite the club's mediocre showing, had established a new club scoring record with 16 games still left to play. He eventually ended the season with 35 league goals and now 67 years later, his total still has to be beaten by a Swansea player in league football.

At the end of the season Pearce left to play for Charlton Athletic but returned to the Vetch Field in 1937, eventually ending his career through injury with the Swans a year later, having scored 43 goals in just 56 first team outings.

PENALTIES
In 1914-15 the League Champions Blackburn Rovers visited the Vetch Field for an FA Cup first round tie. The result should have been a forgone conclusion but Ben Beynon put the Swans ahead just before half-time and they held on until a few minutes from time when the Lancashire club were awarded a penalty. Bradshaw who had scored from 36 consecutive penalties, shot wide and Swansea had won 1-0 to cause one of the biggest upsets in the game up to that time.

In 1933-34, Wilf Milne who scored just seven goals in 585 league games, netted from the spot in the final match of the season against Plymouth Argyle - had he missed, the Swans would have been relegated to the Third Division (South).

One of the most unusual penalties awarded against Swansea came in the game against Middlesbrough in 1956-57. The Teeside club won 6-2 with Swansea-born Bill Harris scoring from the spot after Bryn Jones had picked the ball up in the penalty area after having believed that the referee had blown his whistle!

PENALTY SHOOT-OUTS

Whilst the Swans have been involved in a number of penalty shoot-outs, none were more important than the one at Wembley on 24 April 1994 in the Autoglass Trophy Final. The tie against Huddersfield Town stood at 1-1 after extra time and though the Terriers struck the bar twice and Swansea 'keeper Roger Freestone pulled off an outstanding save, goals from Cornforth, Ampadu and Torpey gave the Swans victory.

PENNEY, DAVID

A Yorkshireman born in Wakefield, midfielder David Penney started his career at Pontefract from where his break into league football came in 1985 when Derby County paid £1,500 to acquire his services. However, first team opportunities were limited and he moved to Oxford United for a fee of £175,000 during the summer of 1989.

After playing in 129 first team games for the Manor Ground club, he signed a contract with Swansea in the 1994 close season, having spent the last month of the 1993-94 season on loan to the Vetch Field club.

An experienced and determined player, he was more than capable of scoring from long range, an ability which brought a new dimension to the Swans' midfield. Following the departure of Shaun Garnett to Oldham Athletic, Penney was appointed club captain and even ended that season of 1996-97 as the Swans' leading scorer with 13 league goals, six of them from the penalty-spot. Surprisingly he was allowed to leave the Vetch after scoring 26 goals in 144 League and Cup games and join rivals Cardiff City where on his arrival he was appointed captain.

A fully qualified FA Coach, the hard-working midfielder was instrumental in the Bluebirds winning promotion to the Second Division in 1998-99.

PHELAN, TERRY

The competitive left-back began his Football League career with Leeds United where he progressed to the professional ranks through the YTS scheme. After two years at Elland Road in which he made 19 first team appearances, he was freed and joined Swansea, who were then managed by Terry Yorath.

During the 1986-87 season in which the Swans finished 12th in the Fourth Division, Phelan missed just one game, playing in 57 matches before becoming one of Bobby Gould's first signings as manager of Wimbledon.

At the end of his first season with the 'Dons' he won an FA Cup winners' medal as Liverpool were beaten 1-0. A virtual ever-present in his five seasons with Wimbledon, he won the first of 38 caps for the Republic of Ireland when he played against Holland on 11 September 1991. After appearing in 198 games for Wimbledon, he joined Manchester City for a record fee for a full-back of £2.5 million in August 1992. He proved to be a real success at Maine Road but after playing in 122 games he was somewhat surprisingly allowed to leave and joined Chelsea, who paid £900,000 for his services in November 1995.

One of the fastest players in the modern game he was hampered by injuries during his stay at Stamford Bridge and in January 1997 he moved to Everton where he suffered from the injury curse which blighted the Merseyside club.

Terry Phelan

PHILLIPS, LEIGHTON

A Welsh Schoolboy international, Leighton Phillips began his Football League career with Cardiff City for whom he scored with his first touch of the ball to draw the Bluebirds level after they had gone two goals down to Rotherham United. Despite playing in a handful of games, it was 1970-71 before he established himself in the City first team.

His performances as a defensive sweeper for the Ninian Park club led to him winning Welsh Under-21 and Under-23 caps before he won the first of 56 full caps when he played against Czechoslovakia in 1971. An ever-present in 1972-73 he went on to play in 216 first team games for Cardiff before joining Aston Villa in September 1974 for a fee of £100,000.

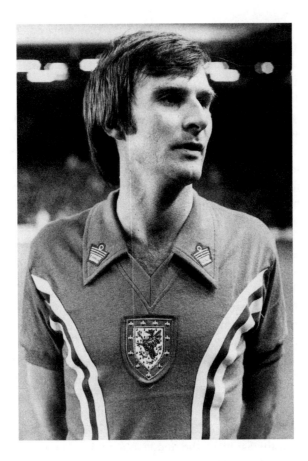

Leighton Phillips

In his first season with the club he helped Villa to win promotion to the First Division as runners-up to Manchester United. He won a League Cup winners' tankard in 1977 as Villa beat Everton, but the following year, the versatile performer joined Swansea.

Phillips who cost £70,000 became the club's record signing and made his debut in a 1-0 win over Bury in November 1978. At the end of his first season with the club, he had helped the Swans win promotion to the Second Division and by the time he left the club in 1981 to join Charlton Athletic, he had helped the Swans into the top flight.

After his short spell at The Valley, Phillips ended his career as a non-contract player with Exeter City.

PLASTIC

There have been four Football League clubs that replaced their normal grass playing pitches with artificial surfaces at one stage or another. Queen's Park Rangers were the first in 1981 but the Loftus Road plastic was discarded in 1988 in favour of a return to turf. Luton Town (1985) Oldham Athletic (1985) and Preston North End (1986) followed.

The Swans have only played on the Deepdale plastic and on their first visit in 1986-87 lost 2-1 with Sean McCarthy scoring for the Welsh club. Alan Knill scored the Swans goal on their next visit in 1988-89 to earn the Vetch Field club a point in a 1-1 draw. The next two seasons saw successive defeats both by 2-0 scorelines before the club's last visit in 1991-92 saw Paul Chalmers net for the Swans in a 1-1 draw.

PLAY-OFFS

The Football League introduced the play-off system at the end of the 1986-87 season. Swansea were first involved in the play-offs in 1987-88 when the club that finished one place above the relegation places played off with the club that finished one place off the promotion places in the division below. Swansea beat Torquay United 2-1 at the Vetch and drew 3-3 at Plainmoor to win promotion to the Third Division.

The format was changed for the end of the 1988-89 season. There was no play-off place in the First Division which meant that four clubs from the Second, Third and Fourth Divisions played off for the last promotion spot.

The format changed again after 1989. All three finals were played at Wembley over the Spring Bank holiday weekend. The lowest division would play on the Saturday, the middle one on the Sunday and the play-off to the top flight on Monday.

In 1993-94, the Swans beat West Bromwich Albion 2-1 at the Vetch but lost 2-0 at the Hawthorns and so failed to reach the Wembley play-off final.

Swansea were also involved in the play-offs in 1996-97 when after finishing fifth in Division Three, they played Chester City. After a goalless draw at the Deva Stadium, goals from Thomas, Torpey and Heggs gave them a 3-0 win at the Vetch in front of a 10,027 crowd. In the final at Wembley, played in front of 46,804 fans, the Swans lost 1-0 to Northampton Town to a 90th minute goal by John Frain.

In 1998-99, the Swans finished sixth in the Third Division but lost in the two leg play-off semi-final against Scunthorpe United.

PITCH
The Vetch Field pitch measures 112 yards by 74 yards.

POINTS
Under the three points for a win system which was introduced in 1981-82, Swansea's best points tally is 73 points in 1992-93 when the club finished fifth in the Second Division. However, the club's best points haul under the old two points for a win system was 62 points in 1948-49 when they won the Third Division (South) Championship. Swansea's worst record under either system was the meagre 29 points secured in seasons 1946-47 and 1983-84. Not surprisingly they were relegated on both occasions.

PRICE, PAUL
Welsh international defender Paul Price who won 25 caps for his country, began his league career with Luton Town but broke his leg twice whilst playing for the Hatters' reserves. He battled his way back and helped the Kenilworth Road club gain promotion to Division One in 1973-74.

In the summer of 1981, Price joined Tottenham Hotspur for a fee of £250,000 but was unable to displace the White Hart Lane club's regular defenders Graham Roberts and Paul Miler. However, he did play in the Spurs team that won the FA Cup in 1981 but at the end of the 1983-84 season after which he had played in 62 League and Cup games, he went to America to play for Minnesota Strikers.

On his return to these shores he joined Swansea in January 1985. The cool, cultured defender was a virtual ever-present in his time with the Vetch Field club, appearing in 61 league games. After leaving the Swans he played for Saltash United and then Peterborough United before returning to non-league circles with Chelmsford City, Wivenhoe and St Albans City.

PROMOTION

Swansea have been promoted on seven occasions. They were first promoted in 1924-25 when they won the Third Division (South) Championship, finishing one point ahead of runners-up Plymouth Argyle. The club then spent 15 seasons in the Second Division before being relegated in 1946-47. Two seasons later the Swans were promoted for a second time, again winning the Third Division (South) Championship, finishing seven points clear of Reading. After relegation in 1964-65 and then again in 1966-67, the club found themselves playing Fourth Division football for the first time in their history. They were promoted for a third time in 1969-70 when they ended the campaign in third place in the Fourth Division, four points behind the champions Chesterfield.

After three seasons in the Third Division, the club were relegated to the league's basement but won promotion a fourth time in 1977-78 again finishing in third place, this time on goal average from Brentford. They were promoted again the following season, finishing behind Shrewsbury and Watford in the race for the Third Division Championship. Two seasons later, the unbelievable happened as the Swans finished third in Division Two to gain promotion to the First Division for the first time in their history.

The club last won promotion in 1987-88 when after three relegations in the space of four seasons they reached the Third Division after winning the play-offs.

PURCELL, BRIAN

Signed from Tower United, full-back Brian Purcell was 22 years old when he made his debut for the Swansea first team on 26 April 1960 in what was the youngest ever side to represent the club. The average age of that team was only 22 and they went on to beat Bristol City 6-1.

The strong tackling defender was extremely popular with the Swansea crowd and was a mainstay of the Vetch Field club's defence for the next eight seasons. Purcell was one of the few players to keep his place as the club suffered relegation in seasons 1964-65 and 1966-67.

Purcell had played in 162 league games for Swansea when he left to play non-league football with Hereford United in 1968.

He had just established himself in the Edgar Street club's first team when he and another former Swan, Roy Evans were tragically killed in a car crash.

QUICKEST GOAL
On 6 February 1926, Swansea beat Wolverhampton Wanderers 3-2 in front of a Molineux crowd of 12,471. Len Thompson's opening goal for the Swans was timed as being after 10 seconds by the referee and is widely accepted as the Welsh club's fastest ever goal.

R

RAJKOVIC, ANTE

Ante Rajkovic cost the Swans £100,000 when he joined them from Sarajevo in March 1981. He made his debut in a goalless draw at home to Bristol City but was clearly not fully fit and only played in one other game at the end of the club's Second Division promotion-winning season.

Ante Rajkovic

The Yugoslavian international defender who had won seven full caps for his country and appeared in 10 'B' internationals was threatened with knee trouble during the Swans' pre-season tour of his homeland but thankfully he recovered.

The strong-tackling Yugoslav who excelled in the role of 'sweeper' proved himself to be one of the best central defenders in the Football League in 1981-82, the club's first season in the top flight, performing with great consistency.

Surprisingly omitted from the Yugoslavian World Cup squad, Rajkovic was unfortunately hampered by injuries towards the end of his stay at Vetch Field and left the club after scoring two goals in 80 league appearances.

RAPID SCORING

Whilst there have been a number of occasions when the club have produced feats of rapid scoring, one of the most impressive occurred on 22 March 1967. In front of a Vetch Field crowd of 6,383, the visitors Stockport County went in at half-time 3-0 up. After they had extended their lead to 4-0 early in the second-half, there were chances at both ends before the Swans between the 65th and 79th minutes scored a remarkable four goals through Smith, Chappell, May and Curtis to level the scores at 4-4. In the remaining time both sides had chances to win but the game ended all-square.

RAYNOR, PAUL

Much travelled player Paul Raynor began his league career with his home-town club Nottingham Forest. A loan spell with Bristol Rovers followed before he joined Huddersfield Town on a free transfer. Injuries hampered his progress with the Yorkshire club and in March 1987 he teamed up with Swansea.

He went on to serve the Vetch Field club for five years, appearing in 228 games before joining Cambridge United in March 1992. During his time with the Swans, Raynor always gave 100% and many of his 34 goals for the club were valuable ones.

After Cambridge he signed for Preston North End for a fee of £36,000 and was a virtual ever-present in the Deepdale club's side for two seasons before rejoining the Abbey Stadium club in a straight swap for Dean Barrick. Excellent at dead-ball situations, Raynor left Cambridge in the summer of 1997 after playing in 142 games in his two spells to play on a non-contract basis for Chinese club Guang Deong. He later returned to Football League action with Leyton Orient.

RECEIPTS

The club's record receipts are £36,477.42 for the First Division match against Liverpool at Vetch Field on 18 September 1982.

RECORDS

League Points	73	Division Two 1992-93
Goals	90	Division Two 1956-57
Win	12-0	v Sliema Wanderers ECWC 1982-83
Goals Aggregate	166	Ivor Allchurch 1949-58, 1965-68
Individual Goals	35	Cyril Pearce 1931-32
League Appearances	585	Wilf Milne 1920-37
Capped Player	42	Ivor Allchurch - Wales

RE-ELECTION

Swansea City have had to apply for re-election to the Football League on just one occasion and that was in 1974-75 wen they finished 22nd in the Fourth Division. Thankfully, the club achieved the largest number of votes of those applying and so were still members of the Football League for the start of the 1975-76 season.

REES, RONNIE

Ronnie Rees began his Football League career with Coventry City and made his debut for the Sky Blues against Shrewsbury Town in September 1962. After that he became a fixture in the Highfield Road club's first team. Equally at home on either flank, he was never seriously threatened in six years with the club and was ever-present in 1963-64.

International honours soon followed and after a spell in the Wales Under-23 side, the winger made the first of 39 appearances at full international level when he played against Scotland in 1965.

With Coventry he won a Third Division Championship medal but after scoring 52 goals in 262 League and Cup games, he joined West Bromwich Albion for £65,000. He stayed for just one season at the Hawthorns and after a short spell with Nottingham Forest, he moved down the league to Swansea City for a fee of £26,000, a club record fee for the Vetch Field side.

This was his final stopping place in league football and though it has to be said that he never really made the impact for which all Swansea fans had hoped, he went on to make 89 league appearances before leaving the club.

Ronnie Rees

REFEREES

When Swansea entertained Cardiff City in the Southern League First Division fixture of 1919-20, Swansea referee D.J.Sambrook had to officiate because of a rail strike - the Swans won 2-1!

On 11 December 1926, a most unusual occurrence took place at the Swansea v Port Vale match at the Vetch Field when Swansea based referee W.R.Harper was chosen to officiate the Second Division clash. Just to show how completely partisan he was, the game ended all-square at 2-2 with Len Thompson scoring both the Swansea goals.

However, when Mr Harper was asked to referee the Swansea v Bradford City game on 21 September 1929, Lachlan McPherson scored four goals in a 5-0 win!

RELEGATION

The Swans have been relegated on eight occasions. Their first taste came in 1946-47 when along with fellow Welsh club Newport County they dropped into the Third Division. They won promotion two seasons later and spent 16 seasons in Division Two before being relegated a second time in 1964-65. The Swans travelled to Coventry City on the final day of the season needing a win and hoping that Portsmouth and Swindon would lose, if they were to have any hope of avoiding the drop. They were well beaten 3-0 by the Sky Blues. Two seasons later the club dropped into the Fourth Division for the first time in their history after finishing 21st in Division Three.

Promoted after three seasons of Fourth Division football the Swans then spent a similar period in Division Three before returning to the league's basement in 1972-73. They had finished 21st in the Third Division with just 37 points.

The club's fifth experience of relegation came in 1982-83 after they gained promotion to the First Division over a period of four seasons. With just Brighton and Hove Albion preventing them from finishing bottom of the top flight, the Swans along with Manchester City joined the south coast club in the Second Division. In 1983-84 the club were relegated for a second successive season and two seasons later finished bottom of the Third Division to return to Division Four.

The club were last relegated in 1995-96 when they finished 22nd in the reorganised Second Division, five points adrift of safety.

REYNOLDS, BRAYLEY

After playing his early football with Lovells Athletic, Brayley Reynolds began his league career with Cardiff City after joining the Bluebirds in the summer of 1956.

Though on the smallish side for a centre-forward, he scored 15 goals in 54 league games for the Ninian Park club before signing for Swansea for a four-figure fee in May 1959.

During the 1959-60 season he scored 16 goals in 37 games but his best season in terms of goals scored for the Swans was 1961-62 when he found the net 18 times in 33 matches. Included in this total was a hat-trick in a 5-1 home win over Plymouth Argyle on 24 April 1962 and the all-important goal in the 1-1 draw against Sunderland which ensured that the club remained in the Second Division after coming perilously close to relegation.

He went on to score 57 goals in 151 league games for the Vetch Field club before leaving to play non-league football.

RICHARDS, STAN

Though he was born in Cardiff, Stan Richards played his early football in London with Tufnell Park before returning to play in South Wales with Cardiff Corries. Bluebirds' manager Billy McCandless was alerted and in 1946 Richards joined the Ninian Park club.

In 1946-47, Richards, who scored on his league debut against Norwich City, scored 30 goals including a hat-trick in a 6-1 win over the Canaries in the return fixture to set a new club record for the most league goals by an individual in a season. In 1947-48 he tended to suffer from a series of niggling injuries and at the end of that campaign in which he had scored 39 goals in just 57 league games for Cardiff, he was allowed to join his former manager Billy McCandless at Swansea.

Though he was still experiencing problems with his knee, the Welsh international who surprisingly only won one cap against England in 1947, made a magnificent contribution to Swansea's Third Division (South) Championship-winning season of 1948-49. He scored 26 goals in 32 games including four in the defeat of Swindon Town at the Vetch. Despite periods when his knees were so bad that he couldn't even train, Richards scored 35 goals in 65 games before being forced to retire.

RIMMER, JIMMY

Southport-born goalkeeper Jimmy Rimmer graduated through Manchester United's junior teams, winning an FA Youth Cup winners' medal in 1964. After making his first team debut for United on their 1967 tour of Australia, he spent much of his time as understudy to Alex Stepney before being loaned to Swansea in October 1973. Harry Gregg, the former United and Northern Ireland 'keeper who was manager at the Vetch Field, improved Rimmer's game before returning him to Old Trafford. Though he only played in 17 games in that loan spell he soon influenced the team's performances, so much so that in February 1974, Arsenal paid Manchester United £40,000 for Rimmer's services.

During his three seasons at Highbury, he showed great consistency and won an England cap against Italy in New York in 1976. He made 146 League and Cup appearances for the Gunners but after a long drawn out dispute with manager Terry Neill he signed for Aston Villa.

He won League Championship, European Cup and European Super

Cup medals with Villa before leaving to join Swansea in August 1983. He went on to play in a total of 83 league games for the Swans before becoming Youth Team coach at the Vetch.

Jimmy Rimmer

RUGBY UNION

Ben Beynon was the Welsh stand-off half against Scotland in the Rugby Union international on 7 February 1920 in Edinburgh and seven days later played at centre-forward for Swansea Town against Queen's Park Rangers.

Gareth Edwards the former Welsh Rugby Union international who signed Welsh League forms for Swansea City during the 1980-81 season had been on the point of turning professional for Swansea when he was 17 years of age. He was an outside-left in the club's youth team but moved to Millfield School where he concentrated on rugby. In February 1981 he also signed non-contract forms for Swansea City in the Football League.

S

SAUNDERS, DEAN

The son of Roy who played for Liverpool and Swansea, Dean Saunders made his debut for the Vetch Field club as a substitute in a 2-2 draw at Charlton Athletic in October 1983. During his time with the Swans, Saunders scored 12 goals in 49 league games including two in a 3-2 home win over arch rivals Cardiff City on 21 April 1984. However, he was not highly thought of by manager John Bond and after a loan spell with Cardiff, he joined Brighton and Hove Albion.

Scoring 15 goals in 1985-86, his first season for the Seagulls, he made his international debut for Wales against the Republic of Ireland in March of that campaign. Towards the end of the following season, he joined Oxford United but at the end of the 1987-88 season they were relegated to the Second Division and he was sold to Derby County.

In three seasons at the Baseball Ground he was the Rams' leading scorer including 17 goals from a total of 37 scored in 1990-91. During the close season he moved to Liverpool for £2.9 million, a record transfer between two English clubs. Despite finishing as leading scorer in all competitions and collecting an FA Cup winners' medal, he made just six appearances in 1992-93 before joining Aston Villa for £2.3 million.

He made his debut at Leeds United in September and played in every other game that season, finishing as leading scorer with 17 goals as Villa ended the season as runners-up to Manchester United. He was top scorer with ten goals including a hat-trick against Swindon Town and in 1994-95 with 15 goals.

At the end of that season he joined Turkish club Galatasaray before returning to the Football League with Nottingham Forest. He left the City Ground in December 1997, joining Sheffield United on a free transfer. At the beginning of the 1999-2000 season Saunders was back in the Premiership with Bradford City.

Dean Saunders

SCREEN, BILLY

Swansea-born midfielder Billy Screen made his first team debut for his home-town club against Aldershot in 1967.

The quick-tackling Screen soon established himself in the Swansea side, displaying the tremendous potential that had persuaded the club to sign him. Over the next five seasons he scored 14 goals in 140 league games for the Swans. His form for the Vetch Field club was such that he earned international recognition, being capped twice for Wales at Under-23 level.

Despite his outstanding performances in the middle of the park for Swansea, he was allowed to leave the Vetch in 1972 and join Newport County. He stayed at Somerton Park for four seasons and scored seven goals in 142 league games before leaving to play non-league football.

SCREEN, TONY

A former Swansea Schoolboy and younger brother of Billy Screen, full-back Tony Screen made his debut for the Swans against york City in 1968.

The tough-tackling defender stayed at the Vetch for seven seasons, though he wasn't a first team regular for that length of time. His early performances for the Swans led to him winning international honours at Under-23 level for Wales. Tony Screen went on to appear in 129 league games for the Vetch Field club with many of his 10 goals coming from powerful long-range shots.

SCRINE, FRANK

Swansea-born forward Frank Scrine began his career as a rugby player but with the oval ball game not being played during the Second World War he reverted to soccer.

Jock Weir, former Swansea scout and a member of the Swans' side in 1913-14 persuaded the young Scrine to appear in a trial for the Vetch Field club and in 1946 he joined the club on professional terms. Replacing Norman Lockhart who left the club in October 1947 to join Coventry City. Scrine made his debut against Leyton Orient that season. In his early days with the club, Scrine was an out-and-out left-winger whose tremendous body swerve fooled many an opposing full-back.

After helping the club win promotion to the Second Division in 1948-49, netting a hat-trick against Bristol Rovers, Scrine had an outstanding season in the higher grade of football and scored the Swans' goal in the 2-1 FA Cup fourth round defeat by Arsenal at Highbury. Also that season he netted a hat-trick in the club's Welsh Cup Final win over Wrexham. It was this kind of form that led to him winning two full international caps for Wales in 1950 when he played against England and Northern Ireland.

After having made a number of transfer requests, Scrine was allowed to leave the club in October 1953 and joined Oldham Athletic. He had scored 45 goals in 142 league games for the Vetch Field club and continued to score on a regular basis for the Boundary Park club, finding the net 21 times in 78 games.

SECOND DIVISION

Swansea have had five spells in the Second Division. After winning the Third Division (South) Championship in 1924-25, the Swans' first spell in Division Two lasted 15 seasons until they were relegated in 1946-47, the first season of league football after the Second World War. During that

Swansea players celebrate after their second goal in a 3-1 win at Preston which secured promotion to the First Division.

time the club's highest position was fifth in 1925-26, their first season of Second Division football.

The Swans' second spell in Division Two lasted 16 seasons with a best position of seventh in 1960-61 but four seasons later they were relegated. There then followed 14 seasons of Third and Fourth Division football before the club returned to the Second Division for the 1979-80 season. After finishing 12th in that campaign, the Swans won promotion to the First Division the following season when a Jeremy Charles goal in the 3-1 win at Preston North End on the final day of the season assured victory and a place in the premier division of the Football League.

After just two seasons in the top flight the Swans were relegated to the Second Division to begin their fourth spell in that section. The Vetch Field club could only win seven games and were relegated to the Third Division after just one season. Following reorganisation in 1992-93, Swansea played in the 'new' Division Two but after four seasons, finished 22nd in 1994-95 and were relegated.

SEMI-FINALS
Swansea have reached the semi-final stage of the FA Cup on two occasions and both times as a Second Division club:

Swansea Town 0 Bolton Wanderers 3 at White Hart Lane on 27 March 1926

The young Swansea side never really settled against their more experienced opponents and went a goal down inside two minutes when Baggett shot home from close range. Joe Smith added a second for the Wanderers after 17 minutes and then six minutes later extended the Lancashire club's lead.

The Swans were far the better side in the second-half but the damage had already been done and though Fowler and Thompson both came close to scoring, they couldn't beat Pym in the Bolton goal.

Swansea Town 1 Preston North End 2 at Villa Park on 14 March 1964

A crowd of 68,000 packed into the ground for the game on a dull, dreary afternoon. Jimmy McLaughlin scored the only goal of the first-half to send the Swans into the dressing-room with a 1-0 lead at the interval. The game turned sour after the break when burly centre-forward Alex Dawson equalised for North End after 71 minutes after the Lancashire club had been awarded a penalty. The Lilywhites' second goal came from Tony Singleton who shot home from fully 40 yards, catching Swansea 'keeper Noel Dwyer unprepared. The Swans then went all-out for an equaliser but it wasn't to be and for the second time in their history, they failed to win through to the final.

SHERPA VAN TROPHY

The Sherpa Van Trophy replaced the Freight Rover Trophy for the 1987-88 season. In their first match, a goal from Joe Allon gave the Swans a 1-1 home draw against Wolverhampton Wanderers, though a 2-0 defeat at Bristol City in their second group match failed to take the Vetch Field club through to the next stage of the competition.

The following season a goal from Bryan Wade was enough to beat Torquay United but then the Swans lost 2-0 to Cardiff City in front of a Ninian Park crowd of 2,986 and so once again failed to qualify for the knockout stages.

SMALLEST PLAYER

Although such statistics are always unreliable for those playing in the early part of the century, it appears that the distinction of being Swansea's smallest player goes to 'Tich' Evans, the diminutive winger who joined the club from Barry. Sadly the 5ft 3ins Evans took his own life following the sudden death of his wife a few weeks earlier.

SMITH, JOHN

Though he played for Queen's Park Rangers during the First World War, John Smith formerly signed for the London club from Third Lanark in April 1919. He scored consistently in his three seasons at Loftus Road, finding the net 66 times in 159 first team outings.

He joined Swansea for a fee of £250 just before the start of the 1922-23 season. Standing only 5ft 8ins, he was fairly short for the centre-forward role but had a most successful first campaign as the club finished third in Division Three (South). Smith was the Swans' leading scorer with 22 goals, netting a hat-trick in a 3-0 win at Portsmouth on 18 November 1922.

The following season he netted another hat-trick in a 5-1 victory over Merthyr Town at Vetch Field on 10 November 1923. It was Smith's way of responding to criticism in the local press that his performances were not as good as when he arrived at the club.

Following the signing of Jack Fowler in March 1924, Smith, who had scored 36 goals in 67 games lost his place and left the club.

SMITH, TOMMY

Tommy Smith joined Liverpool as a teenager and made his first team debut in a 5-1 home win over Birmingham City in May 1963 just a month after his 18th birthday. In his early days at Anfield, Smith was regarded as an inside-left but he soon developed into one of the game's toughest defenders. Quick in the tackle, the fearless Smith won just one England cap when he played against Wales in 1971.

In 15 seasons in the top flight, he played in 632 games and won a glut of medals at club level. These comprised two FA Cup, two UEFA Cup and a European Cup winners' medal as well as numerous runners-up medals.

Undoubtedly his greatest moment in a Liverpool shirt was in the 1977 European Cup Final, supposedly his last game for the club. The popular Liverpudlian appeared from nowhere to head the Reds into a 2-1 lead. He decided to have one more season at Anfield before joining his former colleague John Toshack at Swansea in August 1978.

He made his debut in a 3-0 home win over Lincoln City and went on to appear in 36 league games for the Swans playing just in front of the team's central defensive pairing of Stephen Morris and Nigel Stevenson. At the end of his first season at the Vetch he had helped the club win promotion to the Second Division but in October 1979, his contract was cancelled by mutual consent after an old knee problem flared up again. He then returned to Anfield and had a brief spell as coach before leaving the game.

SOUTHERN LEAGUE

It was 1909 when the Southern League decided to form a Second Division composed mainly of Welsh clubs. Whilst Cardiff and Merthyr were among the founder members, Swansea were unable to join because they had no central ground - the venue that they favoured, the Vetch Field being required by the Gas Light Company for a new plant.

However, following the club's formation in June 1912 they leased the Vetch Field and in 1912-13 began their first season in the Southern League.

The club's first match was at home to Cardiff City with Billy Ball scoring the Swans' goal in a 1-1 draw. The club's first victory in the Southern League came at Ton Pentre and as the season wore on they found themselves well placed, as visitors to the Vetch failed to come to terms with the Swans' cinder surface. Cardiff were running away with the Southern League Championship but when the Swans visited Ninian Park for the return game, they triumphed 4-2 with Billy Ball, a great crowd favourite scoring two of the goals. However, despite a late run,

Tommy Smith

the Swans just missed out on promotion to the First Division, finishing third.

In 1913-14 the club made a good start to that season's Southern League campaign but with success in the FA Cup, where they became the first South Wales club to reach the first round proper, their backlog of league fixtures led to a series of defeats which put them out of the race for promotion. The Swans ended the season in fourth place and though this was a great disappointment, the sacking of manager Walter Whittaker came as a great surprise.

League attendances fell away during the 1914-15 season, forcing a number of clubs like Abertillery, Barry, Brentford and Leyton to resign from the League. The Swans it seemed suffered more than most from the subsequent deduction of points and again ended the season in fourth place.

On 6 January 1919 the Southern League committee decided that the First Division would be extended to 22 clubs - Swansea attracted the most votes and so began the 1919-20 season in the Southern League First Division. The Swans had a number of new players on their books and a new manager in Joe Bradshaw, the son of the former Southern League secretary! The club's first game in the top flight of the Southern League took place at Luton where captain Evan Jones scored the Swans' goal in a 1-1 draw. However, despite a win at Southampton in their next match, the Swans then lost four successive games before beating Cardiff City at the Vetch 2-1. The club continued to pick up points and despite their bad start, finished the season in ninth place.

In May 1920 after discussion with the Southern League, the Football League decided to form a Third Division and so within the space of 12 months, the Swans had gone from non-league football to becoming Associate Members of the Football League.

SPONSORS
The club's present sponsors are Silver Shield Windscreens. Previous sponsors have included South Wales Evening Post, Gulf Oil, Action Service Station and Diversified Products Corporation UK (Fit for Life).

STANLEY, GARRY
Midfielder Garry Stanley began his Football League career with Chelsea after joining the Stamford Bridge club as an apprentice in March 1971. Initially he found it difficult to break into the London club's first team but once he did so, his performances kept him in the side as a virtual

ever-present for three seasons from his debut. He had scored 15 goals in 109 league games when in the summer of 1979 he left to join Everton.

He never really produced his best form in the two seasons he spent on Merseyside and in September 1981 he joined Swansea for a reported fee of £150,000.

After playing in a League Cup defeat at Barnsley, Stanley made his mark in his first league game for the Swans when he came on as a substitute at Stoke and scored the goal that gave the Welsh club a 2-1 win and took them to the top of the First Division. He went on to score four goals in 72 league appearances for Swansea before joining Portsmouth.

He helped the Fratton Park club finish fourth in Division Two before leaving to play in the United States with Wichita Wings. In August 1988 he returned to Football League action with Bristol City before leaving to play non-league football with Gosport Borough.

Garry Stanley

STEVENSON, NIGEL

Nigel Stevenson joined Swansea City as a schoolboy and remained with the club during their dramatic rise and fall through the Football League. He made his first team debut for the Swans in a Fourth Division match at Southport in 1976 and thereafter became an established member of the Vetch Field side.

The tall centre-half was instrumental in the club winning promotion in three out of four seasons and when they played in the top flight his form was such that he was awarded his first international cap when he played for Wales against England at Cardiff. He made further appearances against Scotland at Hampden Park, Northern Ireland at the Racecourse Ground and finally Norway at the Vetch Field.

After ten seasons with the Swans, 'Speedy' as he was known to friends and fans alike, was awarded a Testimonial match against Real Sociedad of Spain, managed by his former boss John Toshack. It was around this time though that he lost his place in the Swansea side and had loan spells at both Cardiff and Reading before returning to the Vetch to complete 259 league appearances for the club.

In the summer of 1987 he joined Cardiff City on a free transfer and played in 68 league games for the Bluebirds before hanging up his boots.

Nigel Stevenson

SUBSTITUTES
Substitute Steve Thornber wrote his name in the club's record books when he came on as a second-half substitute against West Bromwich Albion at the Hawthorns on 25 January 1992. With the Swans 2-0 down, he netted a hat-trick in the space of 12 minutes to give the Vetch Field club a 3-2 win.

SUNDAY FOOTBALL
The first ever Sunday matches in the Football League took place on 20 January 1974 during the three-day week imposed by the Government, during the trial of strength with the coalminers.

Swansea's first game on the Sabbath was the following week, 27 January 1974 when they beat Workington at the Vetch 1-0 in front of a crowd of 6,716. That attendance was more than two-and-a-half thousand up on the previous home gate.

Since then, the Swans have played a number of games on a Sunday but none more successful than the Autoglass Trophy Final win over Hudders-field Town at Wembley on 24 April 1994.

SUSTAINED SCORING
During the 1931-32 season when the Swans finished 15th in the Second Division, Cyril Pearce established a new club goalscoring record. Signed in the close season from Newport County he scored regularly through-out the campaign and netted seven goals in the space of three days - four against Notts County on 19 September 1931 and three against Port Vale on 21 September 1991.With only just over half the season gone, he had beaten Jack Fowlers' record and went on to end the season with 35 goals.

SYKES, JOE
Joe Sykes began his Football League career with Sheffield Wednesday but in five years with the Hillsborough club made only 28 league appearances. The 26-year-old joined Swansea in the summer of 1924 and made his debut at centre-half in a 2-0 win against Merthyr, replacing the injured Jimmy Collins. Standing just 5ft 9ins, Sykes was rarely beaten in the air, whilst his timing was immaculate and his passing outstanding. In Novem-ber 1924 Sykes was made captain for the visit of Brentford, a game which Swansea won 8-0 and went on to lead the club to the Third Division (South) Championship.

Joe Sykes played for the Swans until 1935, appearing in 313 league games. It was a sad day for the Vetch Field club when he played his final game, for Joe Sykes who felt he was too old to continue, was only 35.

After the war he returned to the club as assistant-trainer, later being appointed chief trainer. Sykes was to have a great influence on the club and it was he who spotted Ivor Allchurch playing on a public park and took him to Swansea's manager Haydn Green when the youngster was only 15 years old.

In 1955-56 following the death of Billy McCandless, he led the side back into the Second Division and introduced a number of talented youngsters. When Roy Bentley took over as team manager, Sykes along with Ivor Allchurch remained on the three-man selection committee. In 1966-67 he became caretaker manager but as the season wore on he relinquished the post after feeling the pressure of the team's poor results.

One of the club's most loyal servants, Joe Sykes was a gentleman and one of Swansea's greatest players.

T

TALLEST PLAYER

It is impossible to say for definite who has been the tallest player ever on Swansea's books as such records are notoriously unreliable. Two players certain to lay claim to the title are Walter Whittaker the former Blackburn Rovers and Exeter City goalkeeper who was also the club's first manager and the Swans' goalkeeper Roger Freestone at 6ft 3ins.

THIRD DIVISION

Swansea have had eight spells in the Third Division. The Welsh club's first spell lasted five seasons before they won the Championship with 57 points in 1924-25. The club then spent 15 seasons playing Second Division football before relegation in 1946-47 saw them return to the Third Division. Two seasons later the Swans won the Championship for a second time, establishing a number of club records on the way - 17 home wins in succession, six away wins in succession, the most points (62) which had ever been gained in a season, 27 victories during the campaign and the best goal difference (+53) which the club had ever registered.

The club's third spell came after relegation from the Second Division in 1964-65 but lasted just two seasons before the club dropped into the Fourth Division for the first time in its history. Promoted in 1969-70, the club's fourth spell in the Third Division lasted three seasons before relegation to the league's basement again in 1972-73. After winning promotion in 1977-78, the club's fifth spell in the Third Division lasted just one season as they won promotion to Division Two.

After three promotions in four seasons which saw them play two seasons of First Division football, the Swans suffered three relegations in four seasons, playing two seasons of Third Division football in 1984-85 and 1985-86. After promotion from the Fourth Division in 1987-88, the club played four seasons of Third Division football until 1992-93 when under reorganisation the club became members of the 'new' Second Division. The Swans were relegated in 1995-96 to the 'new' Third Division, reaching the play-offs on two occasions.

THOMAS, DAI

Port Talbot-born Dai Thomas began his footballing career with Abercregan before being given his chance at Football League level with Swansea.

He started life at the Vetch Field as an inside-forward but was soon converted to full-back and over 11 seasons with the Swans was one of the club's most consistent performers.

After being selected for Wales as a reserve on a number of occasions, Thomas eventually won the first of two full caps for Wales when he played against Czechoslovakia in 1967.

One of the game's best club men, Dai Thomas appeared in 298 league games for the Swans, scoring 16 goals but in the summer of 1961 he was surprisingly made available for transfer at a nominal fee and joined Newport County.

The popular defender went on to appear in 58 league games for the Somerton Park club before hanging up his boots.

THOMAS, EDDIE

Eddie Thomas began his Football League career with Everton and made his debut in a 2-1 home defeat by Manchester United in March 1957. The following season he was the club's leading scorer with 15 goals in 26 league games including all four in a 4-2 home win over Preston North End. In 1959-60 he netted 12 goals in 21 games, a total that included a quick-fire hat-trick in a 6-1 demolition of Nottingham Forest. He had scored 39 goals in 86 league games when in February 1960 he joined Blackburn Rovers.

Though he wasn't as prolific in the Rovers' league side, he did score all four goals for the Ewood Park club in a 4-0 League Cup win over Bristol Rovers.

Swansea manager Trevor Morris paid the Lancashire club £10,000 to bring Thomas to the Vetch Field in the summer of 1962 - at the time it was the second highest amount that the club had paid for a player.

During his time in South Wales, Thomas showed an eye for goal but midway through the 1963-64 season, he suffered an injury that was to hamper his progress with the Swans. However, he did return to score one of the goals that helped knock Liverpool out of that season's FA Cup competition as the club won through to the semi-final.

Thomas had scored 23 goals in 68 league games when as 'the old head' of the Swansea side he was rather surprisingly allowed to leave the Vetch and join Derby County for £6,000. Forming a deadly inside-forward partnership with Alan Durban he scored 43 goals in 105 games before leaving to end his league career with Leyton Orient.

THOMAS, GEOFF

A product of Swansea Schools, Geoff Thomas worked his way up through the ranks before making his first team debut for the club during the 1965-66 season. Over the next ten seasons, Thomas missed very few games and always gave of his best wherever he was asked to play.

Capped three times by Wales at Under-23 level, Thomas scored two hat-tricks for the club, the first in October 1972 when the Swans beat table-topping Grimsby Town 6-2. His second hat-trick was also the club's next hat-trick when he scored three goals in the defeat of Doncaster Rovers on 7 September 1974.

During his penultimate season at the Vetch, Thomas, who had played most of his games in midfield, was converted to a sweeper, though it has to be said, not to much effect. Thomas who was a great servant of the Welsh club scored 52 goals in 365 games.

THOMPSON, JIMMY

Born in the Shetland Isles, full-back Jimmy Thompson played his early football with Heart of Midlothian and Leith Athletic before moving south to join Portsmouth in 1906. He played in 158 games for Pompey before signing for Coventry and later ending his career with Bury.

After the First World War he became coach and trainer at Gigg Lane before later succeeding William Cameron as Bury manager following his suspension after a bribery scandal. In 1923-24 his first season in charge, he led the Shakers to promotion to the First Division by 0.02 of a goal over Derby County. The following season the Gigg Lane club finished fourth in the top flight.

In April 1927, Thompson resigned to join Swansea Town, his first duty being to supervise the club's close-season tour of Spain and Portugal where they were to play Read Madrid and Benfica amongst others. Towards the end of his four years at the Vetch, the Swans struggled to avoid relegation to the Third Division and in August 1931 he resigned his post.

He returned to management with Halifax Town in 1936 and in his first season, the Shaymen had one of their best seasons, finishing sixth in Division Three. Thompson stayed with the Yorkshire club through the war years and then resigned at the end of the first peacetime season.

THOMPSON, LEN
Len Thompson had played for Sheffield and England Schoolboys prior to the outbreak of the First World War before joining Barnsley as an amateur in 1917. He turned professional when he moved to Birmingham the following year. He spent three seasons at St Andrews before being transferred to Swansea in 1922.

By the end of his first campaign with the club, he had established himself as the Swans' first choice inside-left, a position he was to hold for six seasons. During the club's Third Division (South) Championship-winning season of 1924-25, Thompson scored four of the Swans' goals in an 8-0 home win over Brentford, tormenting the Bees' defence whenever he got the ball.

When Swansea played Wolverhampton Wanderers during the 1925-26 season, Len Thompson had the distinction of scoring the club's fastest-ever goal when he netted after just 10 seconds of the clash against the Molineux club which the Swans won 3-2. Later that season he netted a hat-trick in a 6-1 home win over Blackpool. He was the club's leading goalscorer with 26 goals in 1926-27 but missed the start of the following season with an injury to his left knee. Shortly after making a full recovery, Thompson, who had scored 86 goals in 187 league games joined Arsenal for a fee of £4,000.

At Highbury, Thompson became the club's penalty king, though he was later hampered by a recurrence of his knee injury and spent the bulk of his time with the Gunners in their Combination side. He joined Crystal Palace in 1933 before retiring from football a year later. He then became reserve team manager of Tottenham Hotspur before becoming a scout for Arsenal.

THORNBER, STEVE
Dewsbury-born utility player Steve Thornber began his league career as an out-and-out forward with Halifax Town but after moving into midfield he began to look more impressive. Able to play practically anywhere, he had

appeared in 128 games for the Yorkshire club when he left the Shay in the summer of 1988 to join Swansea for a fee of £10,000.

On 25 January 1992, Thornber wrote his name into the club's records when he came on as a second-half substitute in the match against West Bromwich Albion at The Hawthorns with the Baggies 2-0 up. He then proceeded to score a hat-trick inside 12 minutes to give the Swans victory 3-2. He had scored 10 goals in 146 games when he was allowed to leave Vetch Field and join Blackpool on a free transfer.

After just one season at Bloomfield Road he left to play for Scunthorpe United but after 91 appearances was unable to hold down a regular place and rejoined Halifax Town.

TODD, KEITH

Welsh Under-23 international Keith Todd made his Swansea debut as an 18-year-old in 1960, scoring the winning goal in a 2-1 defeat of Derby County. The young centre-forward also made the Swans' other goal for Len Allchurch. Over the next eight seasons, the Swansea-born player proved himself to be quite a prolific goalscorer.

He netted his first hat-trick for the club in the win over Walsall on 3 November 1962, his performance earning him international recognition at Under-23 level. Todd's next hat-trick for the Swans came on 7 December 1963 as Swansea beat Swindon Town. That season he scored some important goals in the club's run to the FA Cup semi-finals including two against Stoke City to earn a draw and another in the 2-0 replay win.

Todd's third and final hat-trick for the club came on 26 September 1964 as Manchester City were beaten 3-0 at the Vetch.

Todd, who went on to score 76 goals in 199 league games suffered from a series of injuries towards the twilight of his Swansea career and at the end of the 1967-68 season, he left league football.

TORPEY, STEVE

Islington-born forward Steve Torpey began his Football League career with Millwall before signing for Bradford City for £70,000 in November 1990. He had scored 28 goals in 113 games for the Valley Parade club when Swansea paid the Yorkshire club £90,000 for his services in the summer of 1993.

On his arrival at the Vetch Field, Torpey showed a tremendous willingness for hard work and battled well up front. Despite being outnumbered for most of his time, he ended the 1994-95 season as the club's leading scorer with 13 goals. He was the Swans' leading scorer again in 1995-96 with 16 goals including both in the 2-0 win over his former club Bradford City at the Vetch. Despite these achievements, Torpey was often criticised by a section of the Swansea fans for his lack of aggression. In 1996-97 he was sent off twice and received numerous bookings and at the end of the season which had seen him take his tally of goals to 57 in 204 matches, he joined Bristol City for a fee of £400,000.

Despite scoring on his debut for the Ashton Gate club, he suffered a bad head injury and was forced to miss most of his first season at the club.

TOSHACK, JOHN

One of the greatest names in Welsh soccer history, John Toshack made his Cardiff City debut at the age of 16 years 236 days old when he came off the substitutes' bench to score in a 3-1 home win over Leyton Orient in November 1965. He soon made an impact in the Bluebirds side and in 1968-69 was the Second Division's leading scorer. Having netted a Welsh Cup hat-trick during that campaign, he scored his first league hat-trick for the Ninian Park club early in 1969-70 against Queen's Park Rangers and followed it up with another in the first few weeks of the 1970-71 campaign in a 5-1 win against Hull City.

In November 1970, Toshack, who had scored 75 goals in 162 league games signed for Liverpool for a fee of £110,000. He will always be remembered at Anfield for his exciting goalscoring partnership with Kevin Keegan that carried Liverpool to European success in the 1970s.

Toshack had a similar league goalscoring record at Anfield as he had with the Bluebirds, 74 goals in 172 games, but those statistics only tell half the story. His ability was flicking balls down to Keegan who would snap up the chances. During their time together, Toshack won two UEFA and an FA Cup winners' medal. He was forced to watch Liverpool's first European Cup victory from the substitutes' bench.

Recurring injuries were limiting Toshack's appearances for the Reds and in February 1978 he joined Fourth Division Swansea as player-manager and made his debut the following month in a 3-3 home draw against Watford. Toshack, who scored 24 goals in 63 league outings, bought freely and took Swansea from the Fourth Division to the top of the First Division in four seasons. In fact, in each of their promotion seasons, the Swans had to win their last game to clinch their place in the higher division and succeeded each time.

It all began to go wrong and in October 1983, Toshack resigned, but in a rather strange turn of events, he was invited back by the directors

John Toshack

two months later! The club's results did not improve and in March 1984 came the final break.

Toshack then took over the Portuguese side Sporting Lisbon, where he proved yet again that he had the magic touch. He later took Real Sociedad to their first Spanish Cup success and then took Real Madrid to a Spanish League Championship in his first season with the club.

Despite this, the club sacked him and he returned to Real Sociedad as General Manager. In March 1994 he had a spell as Welsh National team boss but it lasted a mere 44 days and one game. Toshack, who had been awarded the MBE for his achievements in the game, returned to Spain to take over at Deportivo La Coruna, before joining Real Madrid.

TOURS
In May 1923 after the club had finished third in Division Three (South), the Swans became the first Welsh side to tour abroad when they embarked on an end of season tour to Denmark. The Swans later toured Spain and Portugal and played 'unknown' local sides Real Madrid and Benfica, beating the future Spanish giants 3-0!

TRANSFERS
The club's record transfer fee received is £375,000 for Des Lyttle from Nottingham Forest in July 1983. The record transfer fee paid by the club is £340,000 to Liverpool for Colin Irwin in August 1981.

TRAVELLING
Swansea protested to the Football League when the fixture list was compiled for the 1935-36 season, compelling them to travel from Plymouth on Good Friday to Newcastle the following day to compete in two Second Division matches. The League paid for first-class sleeping berths for the club. Swansea won 2-1 against Plymouth Argyle but the next day were beaten 2-0 by Newcastle. Between the two games, they travelled about 400 miles.

On 29 December 1990, Swansea had decided to stay overnight near Wigan to avoid travelling on the day of the Third Division match. Unfortunately, they were held up in traffic on the way to Springfield Park and arrived late, but they did manage to win 4-2.

TURNBULL, RON
After joining Sunderland from Dundee, the bustling centre-forward scored all four goals on his debut for the Wearsiders in a 4-1 home win over

Portsmouth. He had scored 18 goals in 43 games for the north-east club when he left Roker Park in September 1949 to join Manchester City. Hampered by injuries during his time at Maine Road, he signed for Swansea for a fee of £7,500 in January 1951.

He soon settled into the Vetch Field club's side and there is no doubt that the eight goals he scored in 12 games towards the end of the 1950-51 campaign, helped to prevent the club being relegated to the Third Division.

In 1951-52 Turnbull was in sparkling form, netting hat-tricks against Blackburn Rovers on 8 September 1951 and against Rotherham United on 8 December 1951 to end the season as the club's top scorer with 20 goals.

Though he suffered from a series of injuries the following season, Turnbull managed to score 35 goals in 67 games before leaving league football.

U

UNDEFEATED
The club's best and longest undefeated sequence at the Vetch Field in the Football League is of 28 matches between 1925 and 1927. The Swans' longest run of undefeated Football League matches home and away is 19, a total achieved on two occasions - between 4 February 1961 and 30 August 1961 and then again between 19 October 1970 and 12 March 1971. The club were undefeated at home when they won the Third Division (South) Championship in 1948-49 and in fact only dropped one point.

UNUSUAL GOALS
Although all Swansea fans will have their own particular favourite unusual goal, one that was certainly different was by Roy Paul during the club's successful 1948-49 campaign. As a ball was crossed in from the wing, Paul who was standing well outside the penalty area, threw himself forward and headed the ball into the roof of the Port Vale net with tremendous force!

UTILITY PLAYERS
A utility player is one of those particularly gifted footballers who can play in several positions.

One of Swansea's greatest utility players was Harry Griffiths, who during his time at the Vetch Field appeared in every position except goalkeeper and centre-half.

V

VETCH FIELD

Also known as the Old Town Ditch Field, the site was first used by Swansea Villa during the 1880s before being opened as a sports ground on Whit Monday 1891. At that time, it had a circular running track and a grass track for horses.

When the Southern League expanded into South Wales in 1909, the Vetch Field was seen as the most suitable choice as Swansea's ground but it was by then owned by the Gas Light Company who were planning to build a gasworks. However, after their plans were rejected, the new Swansea club which had been formed in June 1912, secured a 75 a year lease on the ground.

They played their first competitive match at the Vetch Field against Cardiff City in a Southern League game on 7 September 1912, a game that ended all-square at 1-1. Throughout that first season, the Vetch Field had no grass and the players had to wear knee pads on the hard surface of clinker. When they embarked on their second season of league football in 1913-14 they were not only able to play on grass but also had a new 1,100 seater stand designed by local architect Benjamin Jones. The stand however, only ran for two-thirds of the pitch and in the corner, a tall Territorial Army drill hall overlooked a small area of terrace. When the Vetch Field club entered the Football League in 1920-21, a small corner stand was erected in front of the drill hall. In April 1921, the Vetch Field staged its first international match when Wales played Ireland.

When the Swans were promoted in 1924-25, the local Vetch Field Infants School was demolished to allow for the expansion of the North Bank and a double-decker stand at the Richardson End of the ground was built at a cost of £5,540. It was opened in 1927 and the upper tier seated 2,120.

During the Second World War, Swansea's ground was used as an anti-aircraft post and after renting St Helen's, the club returned to the Vetch Field in 1944. In 1958 the Supporters Club donated £16,000 to the cost of covering the North Bank and the following year the fans also helped to fund the club's floodlights which were first switched on for the visit of Hearts in September 1960.

In 1974 with the club experiencing financial difficulties, the Vetch Field was sold to the council for just £50,000 despite the site being valued at a later date at £1 million. The club were granted a five-year lease at a cost of £3,000 per year but with the proviso that if the Swans were ever to drop out of the Football League, the Vetch Field would be lost altogether.

Despite having to apply for re-election in 1974-75, the club won promotion to the Third Division three seasons later. Within 12 months the club had gained promotion to the Second Division, but the Vetch Field then became designated under the Safety of Sports Grounds Act, resulting in a bill of £700,000 to cover the costs needed to repair the dreadful state of the ground. In 1980 work began on the uncovered East Stand and was completed in January 1981 at a cost of around £800,000.

During the 1985-86 season, the club somehow survived a number of winding-up orders in the High Court as they struggled to cope with the massive debts from the ground works. Following the fire at Bradford City's Valley Parade, further safety checks led to the closure of the club's West Stand upper tier which was eventually demolished in 1990.

A new ground is being built at Morfa and it is hoped that the Swans will be able to move into their new home at the end of the 1999-2000 season.

VICTORIES IN A SEASON - HIGHEST
In the 1948-49 season, Swansea won 27 of their 42 league fixtures to win the Third Division (South) Championship, the highest number of wins in a season in the club's history.

VICTORIES IN A SEASON - LOWEST
The Swans' poorest performance was in 1983-84 when they won only seven matches out of their 42 league games. They finished 21st in the Second Division and were relegated.

W

WADDLE, ALAN

A cousin of the former England international Chris Waddle, the gangling centre-forward began his league career with Halifax Town before signing for Liverpool in the summer of 1973.

He spent most of his four seasons at Anfield as a deputy for John Toshack or as a substitute, and appeared in only 22 League and Cup games for the club. His only goal for the Reds was the winner in the Merseyside derby at Goodison Park in December 1973 as he toe-poked home Ian Callaghan's cross. After appearing in the European Cup semi-final second leg against FC Zurich at Anfield, he left the club to play for Leicester City for £45,000.

After only eight months at Filbert Street he joined Swansea where he helped the Welsh club rise from the Third Division to the First. In 1978-79 he was voted the club's Player of the Year after he had ended the promotion-winning campaign as the leading scorer with 19 goals. Included in this total was a hat-trick in the match against Southend United on 28 April 1979. At the end of December 1980, after he had scored 34 goals in 90 games he left Vetch Field to join Newport County for a fee of £80,000.

He later had spells with Mansfield Town, Hartlepool United (twice) and Peterborough United before returning to Swansea for a second spell in March 1985. He left league football at the end of the following season, having scored 44 goals in 130 league games for the Swans, his most productive spell.

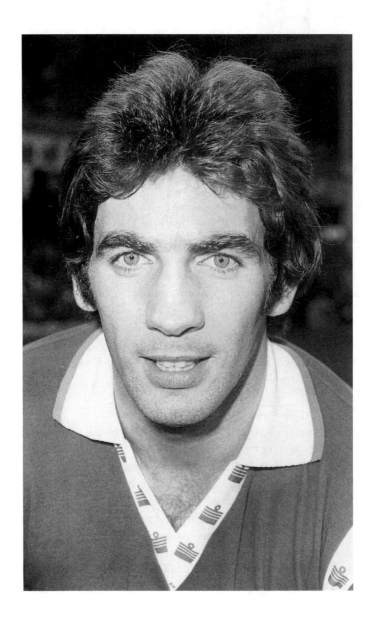

Alan Waddle

WALKER, KEITH

The Edinburgh-born player began his career with ICI in non-league football before playing with Stirling Albion and St. Mirren. Originally a midfielder, he switched to occupying a central defensive position when he joined Swansea for a fee of £80,000 in November 1989.

Since arriving in South Wales he has battled to overcome a series of injuries and his start to the 1994-95 season was delayed by his third hernia operation! However, he is a popular player with the Swansea supporters with his tackling at the heart of the defence, plus his ability to hit his front-runners with long range passes. His bravery and commitment to the Swansea cause was never better illustrated than in the match against Cardiff City at the Vetch on 2 March 1997 when he played for almost the whole of the game with a broken bone in his arm.

This inspirational figure was appointed the club captain for the 1997-98 season, a campaign in which he scored one of his best-ever goals in the televised 1-0 win over Cardiff City. He missed most of the 1998-99 season with ankle problems, but the club captain is hoping to add to his 327 appearances in 1999-2000, his benefit season.

WAR

Swansea lost a number of players fighting for their country. During the First World War, five members of the club lost their lives, notably Joe Bulcock and Ted Mitchell.

WARNER, JACK

Jack Warner, a strong-tackling wing-half was one of the club's most effective performers during the 1930s and in 1937 won the first of two caps when he played against England at Middlesbrough.

During the summer of 1938, Warner who had scored 10 goals in 132 league games left the Vetch to join Manchester United.

Sadly, the war years during which he made over 150 appearances for the Red Devils, deprived Warner of what would have been a distinguished career with the club. He did command a regular place in the United side after the hostilities but after appearing in 118 League and Cup games he left to continue his career with Oldham Athletic. After 12 months at Boundary Park, he moved to Rochdale for what proved to be his final season of league football, retiring at the age of 42. Warner's career spanned 20 years and more than 400 senior games excluding his wartime appearances.

WARTIME FOOTBALL

Despite the outbreak of war in 1914, the major football leagues embarked upon their planned programme of matches for the ensuing season and these were completed on schedule at the end of April the following year.

The club benefitted from the absence of any Rugby Union in the area as the handling game had been abandoned immediately. On the league front, the poor crowds during the 1914-15 season resulted in Leyton, Brentford, Abertillery and Barry all resigning. Unfortunately for Jock Weir, his six goals against Leyton in September 1914 were scratched from the records.

One of the highlights of that 1914-15 season was the FA Cup defeat of Blackburn Rovers in January 1915. The Ewood Park club had won the League Championship in 1913-14 finishing seven points clear of their nearest rivals and were to end the 1914-15 campaign as runners-up in the First Division. A goal from Ben Beynon, the only amateur on the field, separated the sides, Swansea had beaten the mighty Lancashire side 1-0, though Rovers' Bradshaw missed a penalty late in the game. In the next round Swansea drew at Newcastle 1-1 but went down 2-0 at home in the replay. This left the Swans free to concentrate on other competitions. They finished fourth in the Southern League and reached the final of the Welsh Cup where they lost 1-0 to Wrexham at Ninian Park after the first match at the Racecourse Ground had been drawn.

On 19 April 1915 the football authorities finally yielded to the growing pressure and announced that there would be no further League or Cup competitions until the hostilities were over.

Swansea's games in the FA Cup had brought in much needed income to the Vetch Field club and they were also kept afloat by a local league based at factories making munitions whilst a number of charity matches held at the Vetch contributed to war funds. In contrast to the events of 1914, once war was declared on 3 September 1939, the Football League programme of 1939-40 was immediately suspended and the Government forbade any major sporting events, so that for a while there was no football of any description. The Swans had played three league games before the competition was disbanded, winning at Southampton and losing at home to West Bromwich Albion and at Newcastle United where the Welsh club lost 8-1.

In October 1939 the club began to play friendlies and in regional competition but had to move down the road to St Helen's as the Vetch Field was requisitioned for anti-aircraft purposes. Like a lot of other clubs Swansea were forced to play teams made up of a number of young players who were not old enough to be 'called-up', and 'guest' players.

WATKIN, STEVE

Steve Watkin began his league career with Wrexham, playing his first game for the Robins at Torquay United in October 1990 and scored his first goal for the club two games later in a 3-2 win at Gillingham. The following season he scored five goals in the club's FA Cup run including a hat-trick in a 5-2 win over non-league Winsford United and a goal in the Robins' 2-1 third round win over Arsenal. In 1992-93 when the club won promotion to the Second Division, Watkin was the leading scorer with 18 goals in 33 league games.

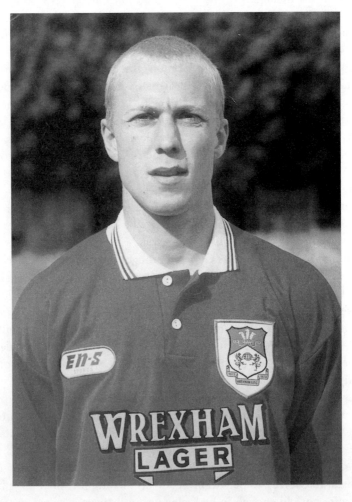

Steve Watkin

A Welsh 'B' international, a feature of his play is his unselfishness in laying on chances for his team-mates whilst he still continues to score his fair share of goals. He had scored 76 goals in 258 games for Wrexham when in September 1997 he joined Swansea. Injured on his debut for the Swans in the 1-1 draw against Leyton Orient he struggled to show his true form and did not score his first goal for the club until 20 December 1997 in a 1-1 home draw against Cambridge United. He has now begun to show the form that made him one of the most popular players at the Racecourse Ground and in 1998-99, top-scored with 17 goals as the Swans reached the play-offs.

WATTS-JONES, BEN

Ben Watts-Jones spent 21 years at Swansea, first as a director and then as Chairman. After helping the Swans into the Southern League he was instrumental in the Vetch Field club gaining entry to the Football League in 1920. Watts-Jones also served on the selection committee of the Welsh FA, but in 1934 with Cardiff City at its lowest ebb after years of success, he was appointed the Ninian Park club's secretary-manager.

After releasing all but five players of the existing staff, he brought in 17 new players. In that 1934-35 season with low attendances and little money to spend, the club finished 19th in the Third Division (South).

The following season was no different as the Bluebirds dropped one place in the league and were knocked out of the FA Cup by non-league Dartford at Ninian Park. He was eventually replaced by Billy Jennings before reverting to his place on the club's board of directors.

WEBSTER, COLIN

Cardiff-born Colin Webster joined his home-town club as a 17-year-old in 1949 but failed to make the grade with them and signed for Manchester United in 1952. On his arrival at Old Trafford he was too old to take part in the club's FA Youth Cup successes and had to serve his apprenticeship in the club's Central League side.

After making his first team debut at Portsmouth towards the end of the 1953-54 season, the versatile forward, who was also able to play at wing-half, played enough games in the club's League Championship winning side of 1956 to qualify for a medal. With United he won four full caps for Wales, the first against Czechoslovakia in 1957, the other three in the 1958 World Cup Finals.

After the Munich disaster, he established himself as a first team regular and played in the club's 1958 FA Cup Final defeat against Bolton Wanderers. He had scored 31 goals in 79 League and Cup games when he joined Swansea for £6,000 in September 1958.

Webster soon made an impact at the Vetch and in 1959-60 was the club's leading scorer with 21 goals. Included in his total were hat-tricks against Plymouth Argyle and Charlton Athletic. The first goal of this latter threesome was scored after just 30 seconds.

He was the Swans' top scorer in 1960-61 when he found the net 18 times but in March 1963 after scoring 65 goals in 159 league games, he left the club to see out his career with Newport County.

WELSH CUP

The Welsh Cup is the third oldest cup competition in the world and was instituted in 1877 with the first final being played at Acton Park, Wrexham on 30 March 1878 when Wrexham beat Druids 1-0.

The Swans first won the trophy in 1913, their first time of entering the competition when they beat Pontypridd 1-0 at Mid-Rhondda after a replay.

In the 1931-32 season, Swansea had to play Wrexham in a Welsh Cup Final replay and chose the day before their final Second Division game against Bury. Nine of the same team appeared in both games which the Swans won by the same score 2-0.

When Swansea won the Welsh Cup in 1965-66 they were involved in a remarkable fifth round match against Cardiff City which went to a replay. The Bluebirds were 3-0 up but in a bad tempered match they were reduced to ten men when Don Murray was sent off and this allowed Swansea to win the game 5-3 after extra-time!

Swansea have appeared in 18 Welsh Cup Finals, winning 10. Below are the years when the Vetch field club have won the trophy:

1912-13	Pontypridd	1-0	after a replay
1931-32	Wrexham	2-0	after a replay
1949-50	Wrexham	4-1	
1960-61	Bangor City	3-1	
1965-66	Chester	2-1	after a play-off
1980-81	Hereford United	2-1	on aggregate
1981-82	Cardiff City	2-1	on aggregate
1982-83	Wrexham	4-1	on aggregate
1988-89	Kidderminster H.	5-0	
1990-91	Wrexham	2-0	

WESTON, REG

Centre-half Reg Weston, who joined the Vetch Field club from Northfleet in March 1945 captained the club during their Third Division (South) Championship winning season of 1948-49.

Solid and reliable, Weston led from the front and during that season inspired his team to a number of records, one of which was to remain unbeaten at the Vetch.

Over the next two seasons, Weston was a virtual ever-present in the Swansea side, Tom Kiley deputising for him when he had to miss the occasional game through injury. However, at the end of the 1951-52 season after which he had played in 227 league games, Reg Weston refused to renew his contract with the club. He had wanted assistance to overcome a housing problem, but the Swansea board refused and he joined Derby County, though he failed to make the Rams' first team.

WHITTAKER, WALTER

Swansea's first manager Walter Whittaker was a goalkeeper who joined the club from Exeter City after considerable experience with Blackburn Rovers.

As he wasn't appointed until July 1912 he had to work fast to recruit a whole team before the start of the club's first ever Southern League season. Also he had to supervise the construction of the Vetch as well.

Towards the end of his first season in charge, the Swans were on target for three trophies. Unfortunately they missed out on promotion from the Second Division of the Southern League but won both the Welsh League and the Welsh Cup.

In his second season at the Vetch, Whittaker's side created more records as they became the first South Wales club to reach the first round proper of the FA Cup. They finished fourth in the Southern League and second in the Welsh League but the Swansea directors thought that Whittaker had not been successful and in the summer of 1914, he left the club.

WILLIAMS, ALAN

Alan Williams began his Football League career with Bristol City and made his debut for the Ashton Gate club at Blackburn Rovers in February 1957. He went on to score two goals in 135 league games before joining Oldham Athletic in the summer of 1961.

Unlucky not to win England Under-23 honours, he captained the Latics to promotion from the Fourth Division in 1962-63 when he was an ever-present. After four years at Boundary Park he signed for Watford but couldn't settle at Vicarage Road and after a spell with Newport County, moved to Swansea in October 1968 for a fee of £1,500.

The strong, rugged defender soon established himself at the heart of the Swansea defence and starred in the club's Fourth Division promotion-winning season of 1969-70. He went on to score seven goals in 145 league games for the Vetch Field club before leaving in June 1972 to play non-league football for Gloucester City. Williams later managed Keynsham Town and Almondsbury Greenway.

WILLIAMS, BEN

Born in Penhriwceiber, South Wales, Ben Williams seriously considered a career in boxing before Swansea offered him the chance to turn professional in 1923. The strong tackling full-back who won the first of 10 caps against Northern Ireland in 1928 went on to make 102 league appearances for the Vetch Field club before signing for Everton along with Lachlan McPherson in December 1929.

After making his Everton debut in a 4-0 win over Derby County, he began to form an outstanding full-back partnership with Warney Cresswell. He captained the Toffees when they won the Second Division Championship in 1930-31. Injured during Everton's 5-1 win over Wolverhampton Wanderers on 24 December 1932, he underwent a cartilage operation from which he never full recovered. In 1936 after appearing in 139 games for the Goodison Park club he joined Newport County and later was appointed chief coach at Somerton Park.

WILLIAMS, GRAHAM

Wrexham-born Welsh Schoolboy international left-winger Graham Williams played his early football with Oswestry Town before being given his chance at Football League level with Bradford City. Towards the end of his first season at Valley Parade, Williams was transferred to First Division Everton and made his debut in the top flight in a 2-1 home defeat by Sunderland in March 1956. However, he was never able to establish himself fully in the Everton side and in February 1959 after scoring six goals in 31 league games, he joined Swansea for a fee of £5,000.

Williams who was known as 'Flicka' was a great crowd favourite and after winning Under-23 honours won the first of five full caps when he played against Northern Ireland in 1961. Fast and dangerous, Williams who broke his leg during his stay at the Vetch, scored 20 goals in 89 league games, a number of them spectacular, before returning to North Wales to play for his home-town club.

He then had a spell in non-league football with Wellington Town before returning to league action with Tranmere Rovers and finally Port Vale.

Williams who scored 47 goals in 249 games for his five league clubs, then joined Runcorn where he ended his career.

WILLIAMS, HERBIE

Herbie Williams was a member of the Swansea Schoolboys team that beat Manchester in the final of the English Schools' Trophy in 1954, a year in which the side won the Welsh Shield. In 1955, Williams captained the Swansea Schoolboys as they won the Welsh Shield for a second time.

After leaving school he was learning a trade at Swansea Docks but decided to give this up on being offered professional terms by Swansea.

Williams was just 17 when he made his first team debut for the club in September 1958 in a 5-0 home win over Sunderland in which Ivor Allchurch scored four of the goals. His first goals for the club came at Leicester City when he scored twice in a 6-3 win for the Swans.

In 1964 he was a member of the Swansea side that lost 2-1 to Preston North End in the FA Cup semi-final and the following season, his performances led to him winning two Welsh caps when he played in both matches against Greece. Seven years later he added another cap to his collection when he played against Romania.

Williams was a great club man and when Roy Bentley became manager in 1969, he was appointed captain. He went on to appear in 513 league games scoring 104 goals including four goals against York City, a hat-trick against Southampton from left-half and a magnificent hat-trick in a 4-0 win over Oldham Athletic during the club's promotion-winning season of 1969-70. Later in his career he settled at centre-half, although he played in a variety of positions for the club.

A skilful and whole-hearted player, Herbie Williams who had played under seven managers, left the Vetch Field in January 1975 to go and live in Australia.

WILLIAMS, RONNIE

Hailing from Trebath, Ronnie Williams made a remarkable debut for the Swans on Christmas Day 1929, scoring a hat-trick against Notts County. The bustling centre-forward was extremely popular with the Swansea fans and ended his first season with the club as their leading scorer. In 1930-31 he shared the distinction of being the Swans' leading goalscorer and also netted his second hat-trick for the club against Nottingham Forest. After that he tended to suffer from a series of injuries, but had scored 51 goals in 187 league games when in November 1933 he was allowed to join Newcastle United.

Though he was badly missed, his performances for the First Division side finally led to him winning international recognition for Wales when he was capped against Scotland and England in 1935.

His stay at St James' Park however was short and after 36 appearances in which he scored 14 goals including a hat-trick in a 7-3 win over Everton at Goodison Park, he left the club.

WILLIS, ARTHUR

Arthur Willis was working as a miner when he was offered the chance to join Tottenham Hotspur. He made his debut for the White Hart Lane club during the war and after signing as a professional, played regularly in one of the full-back positions until September 1947. Despite losing his place to Sid Tickridge, he worked hard at his game and won his place back during the 1949-50 season. He won a League Championship medal as part of the famous 'Push and Run' side and then collected an international cap when he played for England against France in October 1951.

After he had played in 161 League and Cup games for Spurs, he left to follow Ron Burgess to Swansea Town and made his debut against Liverpool in September 1954 in a match the Swans won 3-2. He played for the Vetch Field club for four years, making 95 league appearances and helping them to the Welsh Cup Final in 1956. He was later on the coaching staff before taking over as player-manager of Haverfordwest in the Welsh League.

WORST START

The club have suffered four successive defeats at the start of a Football League season on three occasions - 1931-32; 1950-51 and 1985-86. However, on the first two occasions, the club recovered to end the campaign in 15th and 18th place in the Second Division respectively but in 1985-86, the club finished bottom of the Third Division and were relegated to the league's basement.

X

'X'

In football 'x' traditionally stands for a draw. The club record for the number of draws in a season was in 1969-70 when they drew 18 of their matches.

XMAS DAY

There was a time when football was regularly played on Christmas Day but in recent years the footballing authorities have dropped the fixture from their calendar.

When Swansea played Notts County on Christmas Day 1929, a young centre-forward by the name of Ronnie Williams was given his chance in the first team and responded by scoring a hat-trick on his debut.

The club's last Football League fixture on Christmas Day was against Bristol Rovers at the Vetch Field in 1957. Welsh international winger Cliff Jones, who was later to make a name for himself with Tottenham Hotspur, scored a hat-trick in a 6-4 win for Swansea.

Y

YORATH, TERRY

Terry Yorath's entry into football was quite by accident. He was more noted at school for his ability as a Rugby Union scrum-half and had trials for Cardiff Schools at the handling game. One day he went to watch his brother play football for Cardiff Boys against Rhondda Valley and as the Cardiff team were a player short, Yorath was pressed into service. He did so well that he went on to win four Welsh School caps at football.

After turning down his home-town club of Cardiff City and both Bristol clubs, he joined Leeds United. He had only played in one Football League game for the Elland Road club when he won the first of 59 full caps for Wales, playing against Italy in 1969. Despite going on to play in 141 league games for Leeds he was an often under-appreciated member of the Yorkshire club's side.

In August 1976 he left Elland Road to join Coventry City for £125,000 and in three seasons at Highfield Road he made 99 league appearances before moving on to Tottenham Hotspur.

Keith Burkinshaw had brought Yorath to White Hart Lane to add a bit of steel to a midfield that boasted the talents of Ardiles, Hoddle and Villa. Possessing a shrewd grasp of tactics and an accomplished distribution, he performed admirably for a season but after suffering a series of injuries in 1980-81, he lost his place to Graham Roberts and left to play for Vancouver Whitecaps.

In December 1982 he returned to these shores as Bradford City's

Terry Yorath

player-coach where he helped Trevor Cherry build the Bantams into one of the most improved sides in the country.

In May 1986, Yorath was appointed manager of Swansea and in April 1988 began a successful trial for the vacant Welsh managerial position. At the end of the 1987-88 season, Yorath led the Swans to promotion to Division Three via the play-offs but in February 1989 he walked out on the club to become Bradford City's new manager.

The move sparked off a tremendous row between the two clubs over compensation and the Swans tried to block Yorath's path to Valley Parade with legal action. Yorath paid £18,000 out of his own pocket to honour his contract at Swansea.

Things did not work out at Bradford however and he left in March 1990, returning to his old job at the Vetch within days. He was Swansea's manager until March 1991 and the following year suffered personal tragedy when his 15-year-old son Daniel collapsed and died of an undiagnosed heart condition.

After his departure from Swansea he was made full-time manager of Wales, having run the side on a part-time basis since 1988 but after coming close to qualification for the 1992 European Championships, his contract was not renewed. He is now working in Beirut as the Lebanese national team coach.

YOUNGEST PLAYER

The youngest player to appear in a first team fixture for Swansea is Nigel Dalling, who played in the Fourth Division fixture against Southport on 6 December 1974 when he was 15 years 289 days old.

YOUNGEST SIDE

Though it is always difficult to determine which has been the youngest side that the Swans have turned out, the Welsh club's side against Bristol City on 26 April 1960 contained eight players aged 22 or under and must be a contender for that honour with an average age of 22 years 6 months.

The side was: King (26), Hughes (22), Purcell (21), Johnson (18), Nurse (22), Hale (24), Allchurch (30), Reynolds (24), Dodson (20), H.Williams (19), and B.Jones (18).

For the record the Swans thrashed the Ashton Gate club 6-1.

Z

ZENITH

Though the club have reached two FA Cup semi-finals and recently won the Autoglass Trophy at Wembley, few fans will argue over which moments have been the finest in the club's history.

Though the Swans won the Third Division (South) Championship in 1924-25 in what was only their fifth season in the Football League, the winning of the same divisional title in 1948-49 is arguably the club's greatest moment.

That season saw the club establish the following records:

27 victories
17 wins in succession at home
6 wins in succession away
+53 - the best goal difference the club has ever registered
62 - the most points ever gained in a season (two points system)